Conscious Living, Conscious Dying

Ascended Master Djehuty

Channeled by Tom Jacobs

By Tom Jacobs

Channeled Material from Ascended Master Djehuty

Approaching Love
Understanding Loss and Death
Goddess Past, Present, and Future
Conscious Revolution: Tools for 2012 and Beyond
Djehuty Speaks (a collection of the above books)
Healing Suicide (e-book)

Books

The Soul's Journey I: Astrology, Reincarnation, and Karma with a Medium and Channel
The Soul's Journey II: Emotional Archaeology
The Soul's Journey III: A Case Study
Chiron, 2012, and the Aquarian Age: The Key and How to Use It
Lilith: Healing the Wild
Saturn Returns: Thinking Astrologically
Living Myth: Exploring Archetypal Journeys
Seeing Through Spiritual Eyes: A Memoir of Intuitive Awakening
Pluto's 2012 Retrograde and the First Square to Uranus in Aries (e-book)

Natal Reports

The True Black Moon Lilith Natal Report
Living in the Present Tense Natal Report

Fiction

The Book of John Corbett
Kyle: Theme and Variations
Modern Love: Erotic Vignettes, Vol. 1

© 2014 Tom Jacobs. All rights reserved.

ISBN-13: 978-1497456419
ISBN-10: 149745641X

My thanks go to to Jillian Sheridan for editing this volume. Any remaining errors are my own.

OPENING 6

LIFE 12

SOUL AND ITS JOURNEY 12
THE PURPOSE OF HUMAN LIFE 17
EACH SOUL NEEDS MANY HUMAN LIVES 25
YOUR SOUL CHOOSES YOUR LIFE'S MAJOR THEMES ... 29
THE LOGIC OF SOUL 33
THE NEED FOR A MEANINGFUL LIFE AND WHAT GETS IN THE WAY
.... 49
Judgment, Shame, and Guilt 63
Your Defining Beliefs and How to Change Them 68

DEATH 78

DEATH AND THE MULTILIFE JOURNEY 84
DEATH AS A TEACHER AND NEAR-DEATH EXPERIENCES 95
GIVING AND TAKING BACK ENERGY AFTER A DEATH 100
THE MOMENT OF DEATH 108
WHAT HAPPENS AFTER DEATH 113
Those Who Are Open to Receive Love 113
Those Who Are Not Open to Receive Love 120

CONSCIOUS LIVING, CONSCIOUS DYING 126

PREPARING FOR DEATH BY LIVING A MEANINGFUL LIFE NOW . 128

ABOUT DJEHUTY 145

ABOUT THE CHANNEL 145

Opening

This is Djehuty (a.k.a. Thoth, St. Germain, and Merlin). I am called an ascended master and this is a job title assigned to me in my role as a helper to humanity. I am available to all who ask for my help. My general intention for offering you any teaching is to help you see what you might not yet have seen that can empower you to live in the best possible way. I do this in many ways yet primarily through teaching you to see and read between the lines when it comes to what you have been told and what you have come to think. This is done entirely because it is my role as a portion of divine consciousness to function as a guide for those who seek guidance along all evolutionary paths.

What you will read in the following material is geared toward supporting you in gaining awareness of these topics so that you can see where your choices lie. When you are able to see things clearly you can make more self-interested and self-loving choices, moving closer to embodying consciously your true nature as a divine being, which is to say loving. The intention for offering you this particular teaching is to help you understand more about what and who you are as a divine being living a human life. The focus will be on conscious living and conscious dying.

By the time you are done reading this message you will have insights into the nature of soul, your connection as a human to your own soul, the purpose of human life from the perspective of the creator consciousness of which you are part, and how to move through certain blocks to living the kind of life that your soul embodied here to live. You will also learn how to move toward and embrace death with understanding, compassion, and intention when your time comes. I will share how you can create a life that allows the wisdom and grace of your soul to come through in your living even as you know that death awaits you at some point. When you have read it in its entirety you will be able to see that the relationship between how you live and your conceptions of death and what comes after are intertwined. I will show you how you in fact live in ways that become determined by what you think about death, making your regular experience of life in some ways less about living and more about fearing its end. My aim is to provide you insights so that however you choose to live, you can do so with more conscious awareness about your true nature as a human and all that it means.

I invite you to approach your reading of this message as though it is offered by a kind aunt or uncle figure who has your highest good and deepest happiness in mind, a gentle instruction in something you perhaps have not encountered before. As I come through to you today I want you to be open to the possibility of being helped in altering your relationship with and conception of death so that you may fully live. As you read some of this material it will come in handy for you to remember that as I seek to push your buttons I do so only to be of service to you so that you may emerge on the other side with more awareness of what is really happening on this plane in your human life and how it relates to what is happening on another plane with your divine life. I always seek to add to your human awareness to round out the simply wonderful machinations of mind that you have developed over time. What is not always obvious to humans is the fact that your minds cannot tell you all you need to know. I provide the sort of information contained in this book in order to help you. The help is geared toward showing you that you are creating your reality around you – you are creating your life as you go. It is being created according to the energetic signals your consciousness sends out into the world around you. I aim to make you more aware of this fact but also that you can choose to alter your vibration if you feel that what is unfolding in your life is not helping or serving you. So as you read the material in this teaching I invite you to remain open to learning alternate perspectives that differ – sometimes greatly – from what you have learned about soul, the meaning of life, and the reality of death.

At times you may be challenged as you read. I hold this as indicative of a button being pushed and I know with certainty that if a button is being pushed within you, you are ready to have that button pushed so that something deep within you can come into conscious awareness in order to be resolved or released. You have found your way to this text for a reason and regardless of whether you take in all these teachings and do something with them or not, we are meeting through these pages in order for you to have the opportunity to gain more awareness of how you are wired and vibrating, and therefore why your life is unfolding in the ways that it is. If you read this text and decide that these ideas are not for you, then I will thank you in advance for your time and attention, for your energy spent in giving them a try. My investment is in providing information and perspectives that might serve to help you progress along your divine journey as a human being, and you are entirely free to accept and reject what you will.

If, on the other hand, you begin to take some of these perspectives in and find that emotions come up for you, please know that this is positive even if the emotions are difficult. Channeled material always seeks to alter your consciousness, and yours can certainly be affected even by reading these words – before we even get to the teaching. My conscious intent comes through when people read my teachings, and this is a good thing. It can help you gain exposure to a level of awareness that might not be available to your conscious mind on a regular, daily basis. If you do have buttons pushed when you are reading this material, I want you to be gentle with yourself and take your time to process emotions that might arise as you go. You are an energetic and emotional being, and I would like to put your attention on the fact that your conscious mind – the part of you that will use your senses to consume the material in this book – might not be attuned to allowing the rest of you to process reactions to what you read, in some cases let alone have such reactions.

All of this to say that I would like for you to check in with yourself as you read on to remain aware of what you are experiencing through your body and emotions. They will tell you if something is coming up that needs attention. They will inform you if you need to read the text in measured doses. Some of you will read this in one or just about in one sitting and others will seem to plod their way through it slowly over time, perhaps even putting it down for a long time before picking it up again later. Whatever pace is best for you is what is right for you, and your body and feelings will tell you this even as your conscious mind might want to try to keep going when it may not be best for you to do so.

Let us begin.

Life

Soul and its Journey

The first thing to explain to you is the nature of soul. Human religious and spiritual traditions all seem to have a sense of what soul is about, and these explanations are readily available for you to explore. Yet, to be fair, it needs to be said that some of the groups and traditions producing these explanations have unseen and unnamed agendas to serve by getting you to believe their version of what a soul is and how it functions and, therefore, how you should live your life. Their perspectives are unavoidably shaped by those agendas. When you buy into some of the existing ideas on your planet about the nature and function of soul, you align yourself with what amounts to political aims of a few who seek to control the masses. Sometimes they can be seen to have positive motivations, such as social cohesion and support – but not always. These approaches tend to be something other than empowering because they do not expose you to your true nature as the progenitor of the power of love, a divine being who is part of All That Is or creator consciousness. Some of you are comfortable with the word God and others Goddess, some the Universe, and so on. I tend to use the phrase All That Is to represent this concept yet avoid the political agendas that throughout human history have become tied to the idea of and word God.

Soul is a portion of All That Is. When intact – when all the portions function together as one unit, which is its default mode – self-awareness is not possible. All That Is in this state knows all. It is all. It feels all from all sides and all at once. Perspective cannot be gained and, therefore, self-knowledge is not possible because there is no self to observe and learn about in contrast to anything else. There is just everything, and everything is loving, compassionate, and understanding.

The decision was made by All That Is to learn to know itself. It was clear to All That Is that the only way to do this would be to portion itself off into separate-seeming parts and assume unique identities.

A soul is a portion of this divine consciousness seemingly separated from the rest in order to have a unique experience of self. Yet the only way such an experience is available is through interacting with others. This is to say that soul does not achieve the knowledge of being a unique individual that is desired by All That Is simply by appearing or pretending to be one; it does so by being apparently individual and interacting with other portions of All That Is doing the exact same thing.

Two important notes need to be included before we proceed. The first is that all portions of All That Is agree to forget their true nature ... for a while. They set out to inhabit their human selves fully, including the sense of unique personality possessed by each human that is in fact not the same as their true, divine nature. Each portion understands that it will experience human life through the lenses of their humans' ideas, beliefs, thoughts, and feelings. While this happens, the humans will not remember what their souls – the divine portions of creator consciousness or All That Is – never forget, namely that they are the source of love. The humans will be going about their business thinking they are their names, family histories, professions, relationships, desires, fears, preferences, obligations, and other facets of personality and human life. The humans, for the most part, will have no idea that there is another, true nature for them to remember and reconnect with, living their lives on Earth as if that's all there is to their existence.

One of the reasons it is easy for humans to avoid remembering or bumping into the truth that they are portions of All That Is is due to your anatomy. There are two biological genders, and this fact forms one basis for the observation that it must not be possible that you are all the same. Additional layers with similar themes can be added here to discuss differences in skin tone, intelligence of various kinds, and other features of human biology that set you apart from others in certain ways and can seem rather meaningful. And then there is the matter of conditioning, or training, which makes you appear even more different than others who have even the same gender or skin tone as you, and so on.

The second note is that it is all temporary. The decision to portion itself off into apparently discrete parts in order to learn about itself is viewed by All That Is as an experiment. At times it is referred to as "the manifestation experiment." All That Is asks itself,

"What would be required to learn about myself? What would happen if I were not in possession of all data about everything all the time and all perspectives? What if there were things I didn't know?" All That Is intends to work through all possible interactions of itself with itself as portions of apparently-discrete individuals (humans) forgetting their true nature as the progenitor of the power of love. It recognizes that it needs many sorts of interactions between many sorts of individual pieces of itself in order to learn about all the possibilities.

As you explore your life and those of others in your world, you perhaps cannot imagine the scale of time that is required to complete all of this, but All That Is knows that it is temporary. It – in the form of billions of souls - is watching outside what we might call the game space of life on Earth to observe how its seemingly-separate portions learn about themselves through interactions with each other. We will explore this in the section "Each Soul Needs Many Human Lives," but for now please be aware that the manifestation experiment is temporary and this is so by design.

And so it is that you and all people you have ever met and ever will meet are portions of divine consciousness or All That Is living human lives, seemingly separate from each other and somewhere along a time-intensive trajectory to eventually remember the thing that you as the divine intentionally, temporarily forgot: *You are only apparently separate from the divine. You are a portion of All That Is.*

The Purpose of Human Life

A soul is in the position it is in – living many human lives on Earth, as we will explore below – in order to learn what it means to do so. To learn about itself, All That Is in these seemingly-separate portions called souls interacts with itself while human as though they are not the same thing. Each learns to develop an ego and sense of self, an identity of one kind or another that tells the human person what he or she is about and where he or she is headed and why.

One ultimate goal of all of this is to learn about the power of choice. The original intent is to learn about the self, and this is done by temporarily splitting portions of divine self off from the rest and then interacting with one another to see what happens. Learning to make choices from different motivations is a major part of the manifestation experiment. Dealing with the consequences of choices made from different motivations is equally important.

As you view your life as it has been constructed and developed by you, your thoughts, your beliefs, and your emotions, consider that the essential reason divine consciousness as soul embodied as you is to learn about how to make choices and deal with the results of those choices. When people live in their minds (which are often self-appointed dictators for life), they may come to interpret their choices as meaningful in terms of the factual outcomes of the decisions they make, failing to realize that motivation matters. Your soul is observing and is interested much more in why you choose than what you choose. Your motivation is everything! *Why you do something is more important than the thing being done.*

This is a way of saying that the results of choices are determined less by the facts in play than the energies in play as the situation unfolds. What you-as-soul are really learning is not about the logic, facts, and details that go into making decisions and choices ... *you are learning about progressing from choosing and deciding from a motivation of fear to one of love.*

It is all about the vibration you are emitting. And there are two vibrations: fear and love.

And so it is the point of sentient life on Earth to learn to become loving – to explore fear in all its possible manifestations and then to choose love. Your true nature as soul – a portion of All That Is – is loving and only loving, and your mission as a being with sentience on the Earth is to learn to remember this fact. Each of you cycles through the attitudes, beliefs, and motivations that are modeled for and taught to you before you figure out what it means to be truly loving. Each of you tries to do a right thing with a fear-based motivation because that is often all or most of what you have been shown and taught. As a consequence you learn in hard ways what comes of making decisions and choices from fear. Then your minds come in and ascribe reasons for why the situation did not work out well and this is the source of beliefs that get stuck in your field and float around, creating in the world around you things your personality does not want to experience.[1]

---

[1] If something similar happens a number of times and you are sufficiently injured by it in some way a belief about it can become cemented in your field and this becomes karma, incidentally.

Take a moment to consider choices you have made in the past (whether distant or recent) that didn't work out as you wanted them to. Remember what reasons you ascribed to why it worked out the way it did. Evaluate with honesty what motivated you to decide what you did and see if it was love or if it was fear. If something is sticking with you, it is almost guaranteed that fear was the motivation. Decisions made from a place of love that didn't work out are never those you are bent out of shape over, as it happens – what gets stuck in your field and follows you around is all about what you perceive has gone wrong. When you make loving decisions that don't go well, you can usually accept the outcomes without adopting fear and you can access inner resourcefulness to make happen what you need to make happen. All decisions made from love strengthen you energetically as well as emotionally. All decisions made from a place of fear weaken you energetically and emotionally and, in fact, lead to making more decisions based in fear, and the effect compounds until something tries to break within you: your sense of strength as a human.

If you have been thinking of what you consider failures in your past (whether distant or recent) please be aware of the fact that as beings learning to make choices from the right motivations, you are bound to make what look like mistakes along the way. You are in a long-term, multilife process of learning how to be a person, which is to say how to make choices and deal with the consequences and results of those choices. Put another way, it is by design of All That Is that you appear to mess up now and then! Or perhaps this happens often, depending upon your relationship with loving vs. fear-based motivations ... because if you hold onto fear, then you will generate more fear and draw more fear-inspiring circumstances into your life. If you can find it within yourself to forgive what seem like your failures then you are another step closer to inhabiting your true nature as a divine being who is loving – the basic, fundamental truth about who you are behind this human personality of yours. It is up to you, but I would like for you to know that it is your option to view things that don't go well as failures or as elements in your long-term process to learn about making choices and dealing with the consequences.

In many places I describe this process of learning over the long haul (over the course of many lives) to become the source of love. I have shared that most people are somewhere in the vast middle of the range of this learning curve, making decisions that might not work for them or others as they learn about all that is discussed in the preceding paragraphs. Becoming the source of love is the point of human life, according to All That Is, but never forget that built in is an expectation that many decisions will be made from motivations centering on something other than love. All That Is is not a harsh taskmaster and cruel critic of itself! It is kind and patient; it is understanding and supportive.[2] I invite you to explore how willing you are in this moment to approach your life history of making choices through the lens of kindness, patience, and understanding. As stated above, the more you do this the closer you get to reconnecting with your true nature as divine consciousness, which is loving.

All the things that your mind may perceive are the point of life are, in fact, tools that can serve you in your long-term process of becoming the source of

---

[2] This is reflected in the fact that each human has a team of guides – often called spirit guides – who endeavor to nudge you in the directions that serve you best and, if the human engages them, answer the human's questions about how to live in the best possible ways. Guides have access to the manual that the soul wrote while the human has mostly forgotten that there is a plan in the first place and often cannot read that manual.

love. Many people in various parts of the world perceive that there is work for them to do in the world that is the purpose of their lives. Others perceive their relationships and responsibilities are the point of their lives. This is all fine, of course. That kind of thing is one sort of route to learning about creating meaning for the self, which we will discuss in detail in a later section. It reflects the input of your linear, logical mind attempting to create meaning through material means. Yet behind all perceptions of purpose that are in place because of your mind's input, there is this important, life-changing process of learning to become the source of love. Whatever you do in the world, if your motivation is loving or becomes loving over time, then you are learning what All That Is intends to learn through the lens of your life. Again, it does not matter as much *what* one does as much as *why* one does it.

To be honest about one's motivations – whether fear or love – takes energy, intention, and awareness. In every moment you have choice about how to create this or respond to that. In each and every moment there exists the opportunity for you to be and remain aware of your motivation. I invite you to try an experiment beginning the next time you put down this text and go back to living your life. Look closely at the motivation you have for what you choose to do. Evaluate honestly what decisions you make from a place of fear and, instead of judging yourself for this, be aware that this is part of the process of All That Is learning what you have become human in order to learn. In fact, I want you to refuse to judge yourself but each day and each hour become sensitized to all vibrations other than love that you might work from when preparing to make and actually making decisions and choices about all things large and small in your world. In time you will become sensitive to when a nonloving energy appears in your field and you can alter the course of your life through shifting the balance of decision-making from nonloving to loving motivations.[3] At times it is not easy because you will have to confront the meaning that parts of you and past yous have attached to why you hold onto

---

[3] Also, over time, you will notice the same thing in the world around you, including your relationships. You will serve yourself (and therefore All That Is) well by learning to respond to the fear of others with loving kindness. However, once you begin shifting the balance of fear vs. love within you, the presence of fear in others may make you recoil and you will find yourself judging them. Use these instances as opportunities to exercise your loving-intention muscle in your responses to them.

fearful or nonloving energy. Such inner work takes strength, and I want you to know that as challenging as it gets, you can decide that you are strong enough to do it. Being strong results from a decision to be strong because, after all, you are a member of the creator consciousness club – you are a portion of the divine. Decide to be strong and you will be able to face all that you need to face within that comes up during this self-reflective process.

Each Soul Needs Many Human Lives

The process of learning to become the source of love – learning to inhabit your divine nature while embodied as a human – must unfold over the course of many lives spread out along the Earth timeline. Think about all of the variables associated with your personality and conditioning in this life, and you will see how complex any given human life is. To your mind it may seem that you represent too much data to deal with, but realize that you are just one person! Soul needs numerous examples – humans associated with it – to make a wide variety of decisions and choices from a wide variety of motivations. Some of the variables to do with your life will be certain facts about your personality and conditioning but also how those facts fit into the contexts in which you find yourself in this life. Gender, education level, religious inclinations and refusals, sexuality, and politics are just a handful of the many sorts of facts about you that determine how and why you make decisions and choices. All of these facts and more add up to create certain intellectual, cultural, emotional, filial, and other orientations within your consciousness that contribute to how and why you choose what you do. While you represent a vast variety of ideas, beliefs, and inclinations, being just one person means that your choices inform soul but only as input from a single individual. Soul needs many people associated with it to go through the same exact process as you to learn to make decisions but using different contextual variables such as gender, religious inclinations, sexuality, and others.

Let us say that in one particular life your skin tone puts you in the minority of the culture in which you find yourself. It might serve to seem to limit opportunity in that life. In another life associated with your soul (you have been trained to call them "past lives" but from the soul's perspective, all of its lives are happening simultaneously – soul knows no time), the very same skin color puts you in the majority and you find many more opportunities for success or advancement than in the other life. The same is true of religion, ethnic identity, education level, politics, level of curiosity about life, and all other facts about your personality and conditioning.

One very obvious sort of example that you in your modern ways will not think much of – making it a neutral fact about how a person is wired – is handedness. In your modern culture those who are left-handed are not considered a minority worthy of persecution, but there are spots on the Earth timeline during which they most certainly are. This difference was feared and those who displayed it were at times treated poorly because of it. You can likely accept in your own time that there is nothing wrong with being left hand-dominant, but in some times and places in Earth's history it has been considered so. The same goes for what one eats or won't eat, adhering to any particular religion, having pink or brown skin, displaying or not displaying intelligence, and many other factors of human personality and conditioning.

Soul is outside time observing how the totality of variables associated with each of its human lives – your life being one – contribute to the individuals' decision-making processes and the ideas, beliefs, and emotions that follow the choices based on the large aggregate of variables that make each of the individuals unique. Soul is noting the nuances of thought and feeling that you and all of your other lives associated with it have as you and they observe themselves fitting into or not fitting into the contexts in which each finds the self.

This picture can quickly get out of hand for your linear, logical mind. For now I wish to impress upon you that as complex is your personality and multilayered your conditioning about who you are in your given life, your soul requires observation of many such complex and multilayered human selves in order to learn what it has set out to learn. Instead of making your life simply appear to be one of many (and, therefore, perhaps not that important), it instead means that your life is integral to the long-term process of learning that soul undergoes when it embodies as a human over the course of the Earth timeline. Your choices and decisions – informed as they are by all the things about you that are true, preferred, and perceived – are central to your own portion of divine consciousness to learn about itself through the manifestation experiment. *You are one critical node on a vast network of selves that are each learning what your soul sets out for you to learn.* As we continue with our explanations of these things, remember that you as a unique individual learning about exercising free will and ultimately learning to choose from love and become the source of love are necessary to the process of the entire human game.

Your Soul Chooses Your Life's Major Themes

Your life can be thought of as an exploration of several major and a number of minor themes that unfolds over the time that you live. Each of your soul's other lives spread out along the Earth timeline are to be thought of in the same way. What is happening behind the scenes is that each soul chooses a set of life themes to explore over the course of many lives as the vehicles for learning to make choices and deal with the results (as described above) in order to learn to turn fearful motivations into loving ones. And so it is true that the major themes of your life are in common with other lives that your soul is living elsewhere on the Earth timeline. Your soul is observing how the same themes are approached by its manifestations in a variety of lives defined by the numerous variables of personality, genetics, and conditioning (as explored in the previous section).

Whatever the life theme, it is approached by numerous manifestations of the soul (you and your soul's other lives) within many different contexts. In some lives the theme is explored when there is a lot of money and resources available to the person and other lives when there is not. With the same person the theme chosen by his or her soul is played out when the person's skin color puts him or her in the majority and perhaps leads to privilege and in other lives in the minority, which perhaps leads to less or a lack of privilege. That very same theme in some lives is explored by humans as men and in other lives as women, as homosexual and heterosexual, smart and not so smart, trusting in life and not trusting in life, and so on.

When your conscious mind begins to grasp the enormity of what is going on from the point of view of soul, it can begin to get a little overwhelming. Your linear, logical mind is not outfitted by default to be able to work with such a high number of variables, and so it is important to note that you need not work with or hold all of them in conscious awareness at the same time. What matters is this:

As your life revolves around certain major and minor themes, all of your soul's lives revolve around those same themes. The themes are approached by the different manifestations of your soul in different ways using different personalities and conditioning. This is so that soul can experience the wide variety of examples of humans exploring that theme so that it can learn as much as possible about how and why humans make choices and, ultimately, learn about becoming the source of love.

Consider what seem major themes in your life. Perhaps you have a thing about safety and security or a need for respect. Perhaps you feel urgency about expressing creativity or your ideas. Or maybe you know about yourself that you have a hard time making the right choices for yourself and/or accepting that everything works out in the end. It could be instead that you are seeking something from others that seems impossible to find. Think of the content of your emotional life – what seems to weigh on you persistently and be on your mind and in your heart that might not ever feel fully resolved – and, chances are, you are looking at at least some of the major themes your soul has set out for you to teach it how and why a person makes choices.

You can also view your thoughts and feelings about your genetics or background (ethnic, religious, national, etc.), and they will tell you something about these themes set out for you by your soul. Whatever it is that's in your life, including early-life experience and conditioning, indicates what has been set out by soul for you as a human to explore in order to learn to make choices and deal with the results. Another layer of this is to view your reactions to any and all contexts from past and present that have shaped or are shaping you now. These thoughts, feelings, and reactions will also tell you about what your soul has set out for you. Essentially, if it is important and formative for you, your soul has set that in motion so it can learn through how you express your free will and deal with the results of those choices.

It is at this point that I wish to point out to you that this includes the areas of life and situations to which you have deep and abiding aversion. All that is in your life that stays or lingers represents experiences by which your soul intends that you become confronted so that you have opportunities to learn to make the right sorts of choices in response. For the most part, humans do not like to feel pain and so will avoid it, but it's also true that things that confuse you create tension that can turn into pain. So even if you are willing to be aware of painful situations in order to work through them, how long are you willing to exist within the tension of confusion that creates ongoing and deepening pain? Not many of you are willing to do this before really getting just how important it is to work through what is painful. To create willingness to do so, it is important to understand the logic according to which your soul operates, which determines much of what comes to you in life.

The Logic of Soul

What you experience in your life that relates to major and minor themes – the things that are repeatedly or continually on your mind and heart – are, in a sense, energetically coded in you by soul. The portion of divine consciousness that is yours sets into motion certain vibratory states within you that it knows will manifest in your life. As stated above, when All That Is is intact, it cannot know itself, and so the decision was made to portion pieces of itself off in order to create and learn through experiences based in a perception of separateness. As you are one of these pieces, you are vibrating what we should consider divine commands. It is these elements of your energetic field that draw to you the experiences you have that shape you. Soul intends that you focus repeatedly or continually upon certain life themes available to humans and (as it is the divine) its intentions are broadcast to the universe as commands to bring manifestations of those themes to you. Because of your soul, you are vibrating divine commands that will draw certain kinds of experiences and dynamics to you. Many people notice this effect and wonder if (or assume it to be) destiny or fate. Nothing is predetermined for you except that soul is vibrating through you certain life themes into manifestation around you. How you respond to what comes to you is everything, as I will continue to explore throughout the remainder of this text.

The logic of soul becomes apparent through your experiences. What your portion of All That Is – your soul – sets out to learn through you will, in fact, come to you. This cannot help but happen because the universe is responding to your divine command! As a portion of All That Is, you are in fact a portion of the creator energy. What you-as-soul say goes – what you-as-soul vibrate manifests. The manifestation experiment that set the stage for all life required that you-as-the-divine forget this aspect of your creative power and so you-as-a-human have done so. But it is true that your intentions create your reality, and this is true both of your soul and your human self. Perhaps as you navigate metaphysical or new-age teachings you have heard that you are creating your life, and you can be sure that it's true.

By deeply getting how all of this works, you will begin to see how to make your day-to-day, human life align more with soul and its divine commands to improve your quality of life and your sense of belonging here on Earth and having an important, divine mission. Until humans understand all of this, confusion about why things happen to them crops up left and right. The confusion becomes painful as they begin to perceive that they are at the mercy of these unseen and unknowable forces. But they *are* knowable and this is why we are here together today – you are learning how to understand what is really going on in the game space of life for you as a human, why it is happening, and what you can do about it as a divine being remembering the power of free will and learning to be motivated by love.

Back to our story: Soul knows that some of what you vibrate into your life will be painful. It recognizes that painful experiences are just as valuable as pleasurable experiences when it comes to learning about life and all of its possibilities. And so the determining factors of soul's day-to-day involvement in your life are not exclusively about happiness, safety, joy, security, or other wonderful things that your mind may perceive are the right things for you. All humans experience pain and no one gets a free pass! You know this to be true through observation of your life and those of others, but the reason for it has mostly escaped you. The logic of soul is the answer because it is the logic of the divine, which is what you are as you live your human lives, creating the world into existence around you so that your soul – your very own portion of All That Is – can learn what it means to be human, make choices, and turn your life from being motivated by fear to motivated by love.

The logic of soul, the logic of the divine. You may think these are phrases easy to be thrown about by a being such as myself. You might be thinking something like, "Djehuty, you are not living my life.

You have not seen what I have seen. You are not hurt by the past as I am hurt by it. You are not dealing every day with this trouble and that pressure, this tension and that dilemma. You do not have to go from one rock-and-hard-place combo to another for years at a time." But as a teacher coming through a channel to share with you insights into the big picture so you can understand more about what is happening on the Earth plane when it comes to life, soul, and – we will get there – death, I ask you to please be open to receiving this information in the helpful spirit in which it is intended. Please give me the benefit of the doubt even if you feel a bit challenged now and then. As I mentioned in the opening, there may be some material here that pushes a button or two inside you and there may at times be a reaction to what I am sharing with you. At this point please know that if you are feeling stirred to think something like what I have said above, then you have a button that is being pushed. Let this be okay and know that it is temporary. If you resist the notion that your soul accepts painful experiences as part of the learning journey it must go through in order to learn how to be human and how to make choices and learn to become the source of love, then there are some things out of balance in your field that require rebalancing, which you usually call healing. I am doing what I can in this text to provide you with tools to enable that kind of healing and, for this reason, I am glad that you and this book have found each other.

(You are in the same boat as everyone else who is reading this text, as it happens. And, for what it's worth, I've lived a number of human lives and so have been there, too. All those taking on the title of Ascended Master have lived numerous human lives on Earth. We couldn't really help you if we had not gone through the same process that you are going through now, could we? It would be disingenuous to talk at you what we say are truths if we had not lived lives just like yours and come out the other side with more awareness of how all of this really works.)

Each and every human's long-term, multilife journey includes the soul setting out for him or her painful experiences in order to learn about all the possible permutations of the power of choice given the wide variety of contexts and variables in play in that person's life at any given time. Being pushed into pain is part of the divine play, we could say. It is not about pain, to be sure. It is not even half about happiness and half about pain – there is no such divinely-commanded ratio. It is not the amount of happiness or pain in your life that matters to soul but the experience and process of turning fear into love, which can also be thought of as turning pain into love. The quality of your life experience does matter to your soul – and, therefore, to All That Is – but it is up to you as a portion of All That Is to create loving states that feed and nurture your sense of being human and propel you to give to others and the world the gift that you are as All That Is. This is your power. Your soul has not set out to shepherd or direct you but to provide you a sense of strength to learn to make the right decisions for yourself at the right times and for the right reasons. You can choose to connect with and inhabit that sense of strength or not – it is entirely up to you. All paths, in time, teach the divine what it embodies to learn.

If you are someone who has been taught or has somehow come to think that soul is or should be your protector – or perhaps even an older sibling keeping you out of trouble and teaching you the right way to live – it is time for you to update this conception. Soul is divine power not incarnated and you are its manifestation, meaning that you are divine power incarnated. This is not to puff or pump you up. It is not to blow smoke in your direction or to try to get you to try on for size a measure of megalomania. *It is meant to reveal to you that what you are vibrating is just as powerful as All That Is – divine source – vibrating the universe into existence.* You are vibrating your world around you into existence at this very moment, and you always have been doing so. It is your nature to create – you cannot help but do so. While you are in human form, it happens as experiences, situations, and relationships coming to you that manifest what you are thinking and feeling, including what you have thought and felt long ago and in other lives. Your life is a creation of your beliefs, thoughts, attitudes, and ultimately also your worries, fears, passions, and strengths. All that is happening to you is your creation. When you truly grasp this, your life will truly change. You will see that you have been in the driver's seat of your life the entire time but that you have not been aware of how this stuff works. You will be able to begin a new chapter by unwrapping a new map for your life defined by empowering intentionality and, most importantly, setting off in a new direction knowing that you will get there.

The logic of soul says that whatever you-as-a-human need to experience in order for All That Is to learn about what it means to be human is what you will experience. As stated above it is not about pain, but it is equally not about the avoidance of pain. All manner of human experiences will come to you over the course of your many human lives spread out along the Earth timeline. The themes chosen by your soul for you to experience are brought to life in myriad ways across the timeline, yet in any given life you will not experience all of them. A human life is not long enough to sample all the possibilities available to a human given any particular life theme.

Consider the theme of belonging and acceptance. Possibilities include exploring being accepted by familial, community, home, national, ethnic, and religious community. It is possible to have some lives in which each of these is experienced as accepting or not accepting, but to really get into the deep feelings the human will feel when acceptance is not on the table in such contexts needs more than one life to unfold. And if you remember what I stated earlier, it is in the varied contexts with multiple differing variables between separate lives that provide the true learning required by soul, which is to say All That Is.

For instance, if a person feels unaccepted by his or her family in a given life, it could be that the person ends up choosing to set off on his or her own. It could also be that the family throws the person out for some reason. It could happen instead that the person stays with the family but must sacrifice something important about his or her self-expression or values in order to do so. These are just three possibilities that might be explored in a given life. While often situations like this unfold in related stages (after one thing is tried and found not to work, then another is tried, etc.) it is not possible for the myriad possibilities to be explored by any one person in his or her life.[4] Add to this the need soul has to observe what choices a human would make if blue-skinned in a green-skinned world, trisexual in a bisexual world, poor in a rich world, and so on. The variations are limitless, and a wide variety of them need to be observed by each soul regarding its chosen themes in order for All That is to sufficiently learn what it has set out to learn via the manifestation experiment.

---

[4] Sometimes a given life contains many opportunities to revisit the past, and this means encountering many such stages, leaving one to perceive that a lot of past tensions and things left unresolved are being presented to him or her.

The logic of soul says that what you are vibrating will manifest. A detail to mention is that your emotional body connects all of your soul's lives together. What is happening to one person associated with your soul on one part of the Earth timeline can take up enough space in that person's emotional consciousness to affect other people associated with that soul. This is to say that the deeply joyful and deeply painful experiences of your soul's other lives affect you and vice versa. Your conscious mind might not readily accept that it is logical that you must in this life deal with painful experiences that haven't happened to you. This would be entirely normal because your conscious mind is only just now becoming aware of the fact that you are not the particular body, name, personality, preferences, dreams, and fears that you believe make up who you are. Your conscious mind is getting a wake-up call through this text to adapt to the idea that it is an important advisor and integral to your life but not all that you are. Why should you have to deal with the imprints of pain that other humans elsewhere on the timeline have experienced? The answer is that you are a divine being living multidimensionally and now being clued into the fact that you exist across time and are, in fact, immensely powerful as a portion of All That Is.

Some of these imprints from elsewhere on the timeline that are showing up in your emotional body are vibrating to the extent that they manifest in this life you are living. This is to say that some of the joy and pain from your soul's other lives is strong enough to bleed through and manifest in this life. You will, in other words, have some experiences in your present life that are echoes of what is happening to other manifestations of your soul elsewhere on the timeline. Painful experiences can be so deeply scarring on the emotional body that they show up in each life. Now, it is possible that this does not always happen but it can.

It also happens that a person can possess a fear out of all proportion to his or her biography, and this would represent a pain from another life that has perhaps not manifested. You are not in any given life subjected to all painful experiences from your soul's other lives becoming manifest. It would not be possible under those circumstances to learn anything as a human because you would be overwhelmed and not be able to see that you can make choices in response to the situations. If inclined to feeling powerless or a bit of a victim, you would likely crumble under the pressure of awful things happening to you. As it is, you are vibrating into existence echoes of other-life fear, pain, joy, and triumph in measured doses to give you opportunities to respond to them and, in the process, learn to turn fearful and pained motivations into loving motivations.

You are often occupied with the results of what you are unwittingly manifesting. This looks like being happy or unhappy, feeling safe or afraid, or any other emotion with charge that relates to an external circumstance of your life. All of this takes up time and energy and represents the day-to-day learning of All That Is through your human life. Once you are able to see that all that you are experiencing is in fact a creation of your energy field – including thoughts, emotions, and beliefs – you can turn your attention to adapting your human will with your divine will. The logic of soul then becomes apparent to you as you live your life and accept with graciousness that what comes to you is in your life for a reason and that even if the experience is painful, the reason is a good reason: *All That Is needs you to make a decision about how you will behave in response to the situation coming to you or taking shape in front of your eyes.*

The more you are occupied with the results, the more you are in states of feeling without understanding. The more that you spend time in such states, the more that you can get lost in them. This is fertile ground for negative and victim state-inspired thoughts, feelings, and beliefs to become generated and ultimately cemented in your field. And whatever it is that is cemented in your field begins to manifest in the world around you, bringing into manifestation more examples of what hurt you in the past. This is the nature of karma – deep beliefs cemented in your energetic field about what has happened attached to the feelings resulting from the thing happening – and it is the nature of your energetic field to make apparent what is out of balance or out of place. And so it is that your life can be seen as a series of karmic bubbles floating to the surface of conscious awareness but only through becoming manifest in the life around you. If you carry a belief or thought you will manifest it, and very often it is true that you cannot know what you are carrying until it manifests around you.

It is easy for you to use this manifestation process to reinforce what was believed in the first place. You suspect that something not-happy is true and then some version of it happens in front of your face. You take the opportunity to say, "See?! I knew something like that was going to happen. I was right all along!" The purpose of this section of the book is to hammer home the perspective that what you experience is being created by what you are vibrating. Given this truth, my questions to you are, "Well, what do you choose now to believe? What do you choose to think? What are you interested in vibrating into existence now?"

I challenge you to commit to a process of evaluating what you believe as well as what you think it means that certain scenarios present themselves regularly in your life. I challenge you to develop and cement the perspective that what comes to you serves you because it is vibrating itself into existence in order to serve you as you become aware of the energies – including thoughts, feelings, and beliefs – that you are carrying. The most persistent patterns of things coming to you – those that can vex you and inspire you to want to throw your arms up into the air – are those most deeply painful and/or not yet understood. If you commit to seeing all that comes to you as serving your highest good as All That Is exploring what it means to be human, you will be on your way to aligning more with soul. Be sure to remember that soul does not have the job of making life easier for you. You have the job of learning to bring the wisdom of soul out into the world around you. This will create you consistently to be loving – honoring and bringing through soul's true loving nature as All That Is into the manifest world – and will enable you to be able to confront and process what in your life has been the most painful, difficult, and vexing.

And finally, I invite you to embark upon a process of rewriting the history you have attached to your experiences and your past. Using the information contained here about the logic of soul, you can begin to view past experience in a new light. When you can go through your history and review potential reasons you might have manifested what you have experienced, you can begin to release deep and numerous fears that you might carry now about past awful things repeating themselves. You can also begin the process of forgiving all those who have hurt you and forgive yourself for having made choices that seemed not to be best for you or that hurt or damaged you in one way or another. History is a narrative applied after the fact to a series of interrelated events that seem to have lead to this or that outcome. As a narrative it is unavoidably informed by the beliefs, thoughts, expectations, feelings, and individuality of the narrator. If, for example, you were hurt in some way when you were a child, the narrator who has determined the meaning of that painful event is the age at which you were hurt. Now in your adulthood you have the opportunity to go through these files in your head and heart in order to upgrade the version of events to reflect your growing comfort with the logic of soul. After all, if it happened to you it happened for a reason and that reason has everything to do with what your soul – your very own portion of All That Is – came here to experience in order to learn about what love is, where it comes from, and who's responsible for giving it to whom along its path of learning to become the source of love while living a human life.

The Need for a Meaningful Life and What Gets in the Way

Beneath the experience of dealing with the emotions and beliefs that result from what manifests around you, there is in each of you a sense of needing meaning. There is an urge in each and every human to live a meaningful life. In some this is phrased to be about making a difference in or leaving a mark upon the world or, even broadly put, as leaving a legacy. In some it comes out as an impulse toward serving others and in others an impulse to change society for the better in some way. A truth to share with you is that beneath the feelings, thoughts, beliefs, emotional debris, and egoic desires of every person is a powerful urge to be of service in some way to all other beings. Beneath elements of personality within each of you is a vibratory resonance with the fact that you are all the same and that your true nature is to be loving, which is to say giving.

Many of you search for meaning in the world around you. In fact, many of you spend numerous lifetimes on Earth looking for it outside you. If you have not yet realized the truth of it, I would like to share with you that there is no meaning to be had in the world around you. Meaning can only be generated by you. Living a meaningful life is possible for you only if you choose to create the world around you in intentional ways.

Religion and other philosophy-based pursuits occupy a great many of you as you attempt to meet this innate need. Humans can be very clever when putting together images and visions of what life is really about, who your gods are and what they want, and what is right and wrong. You have been consuming these messages for millennia from others who are sometimes well-meaning and sometimes not so well-meaning. In the time in which you are reading this, you are invited to connect to a direct source of meaning, one not explained to you by another person or a book. You have grown out of the many ideas and notions about what is true about life, the world, divinity, and each other that have saturated your many lifetimes on Earth. Now you are reaching out to find what is truly and deeply meaningful. And I am here to tell you that it can only be found within you and brought out. It can be created only through your own creation.

As you learn the logic of soul and begin to see your past and present circumstances in new ways, you will be able to see all of them as your creation. So, in fact, you are already creating left and right! You are already living out your divine nature as All That Is by vibrating an experience of yourself, life, the world, and others into existence. The missing piece for many of you is the part about your creation being meaningful and if you follow the invitations and challenges I am laying out for you in this text, you will enable yourself to see it how to make this happen intentionally so that meaning is in fact created.

Regarding making a difference in the world, you will find – after self-reflection that digs down into how you are wired, how your beliefs shape your vibration now – that there are opportunities to change what you are vibrating. As mentioned briefly above, creating meaning is in creating the world into existence around you with conscious intention. It is in this way that you can participate with awareness in the process of creation, and it is this participation that will bring a sense of meaning to your life. There are those of you who find meaning in being of service, making something better in the world, etc., yet at some point you are each drawn into an interior process sometimes called "soul searching" that is meant to put you more in touch with why you are living – what you really want to be doing with your time and energy. This is to say that even those of you who seem to be creating meaning in an external way that serves you well will each, at some point, be nudged or drawn to the internal side of it. This is a device of soul to cause you to confront the motivations you have now and perhaps have always had. This is the process by which you find your thoughts and attention turned on the role you have had in how your life has unfolded. This is a wonderful chance to rewrite the history of why you have experienced what you have and many who go through such an internalizing process emerge on the other side with the skill of forgiveness strongly centering them going forward. It can be a crisis that inspires such an internal process, but I am letting you in on all of these things so that you can alter your life for the better with perhaps less drama, chaos, and pain than if you were lead there by a crisis of one sort or another. Of course, it is up to you how you get there! Some of you will find that you simply cannot focus on the internal unless something has gone wrong and this is, of course, fine. You are free to do what you must, and my role here is simply to provide as much information and insight as possible so that the choices you are making for yourself can be well-informed given the truth about how all of these things work behind the scenes, which is not always obvious to your human mind and senses.

    You cannot escape the need for a meaningful life. This urge and need will never leave you. There is no remedy for its pulsing, driving existence other than to choose to do something about it. There are those of you who sense a lack of meaning in your lives and perhaps do not know to create something or feel you cannot or should not do so. Some of you find that you turn to behaviors, patterns, and choices that are in the end self-destructive. You might have done this as a distraction or to fill a sense of emptiness that you feel at some point or perhaps have always felt. Whatever your motivation, trying to fill a sense of emptiness with a product, feeling, or interaction will never truly do so. If you go down this road, then you are going to at some point find that it does not work for you. Some of these avenues lead to addictions of various kinds, whether involving substances, experiences, and/or interactions with others. None of them can possibly give you the meaning that you seek. The only way to experience meaning is to create it for yourself. And the only way to do this is to intentionally direct the energies you are emitting and broadcasting that in fact create your experience and shape your life. Attempting to fill a sense of emptiness will lead to more emptiness because what you use to attempt to fill it will be consumed or will go away. It will never be enough.

If this section in general and the above handful of paragraphs specifically resonate for you, I would like to at this point invite you to be aware of judgments you may have about these parts or chapters of your life. If you have turned to substance, things, and/or people to fill a sense of emptiness in you and found yourself navigating an addiction, I want you to begin to frame these choices in terms of the long-term journey of your soul learning how to live life as a human. Consider that this is an experience that All That Is is exploring on its long, multilife, and sometimes convoluted path to become the source of love. When an emptiness is felt and attempts are made to fill it, it is in fact a survival strategy – one that has to do with emotional survival. No human can persist in a state of emptiness without doing something about it. As All That Is seeks to learn to become the source of love, it must through its many human lives lived all across the Earth timeline explore all manner of sides of the experience of learning about what love is, where it comes from, and who's responsible for giving it to whom. This necessarily includes feeling a distinct lack of love from the world around one and a limit to or dearth of the sense of being able to generate love. A sense of not feeling loved and supported can, for many, become chronic.

Something is reached out for as a remedy by many when this feeling gets to this stage.

An urge to fill the sense of emptiness – the hole within that is the feeling of a lack of meaning, a lack of support, and a lack of love – is being explored by many humans all along the Earth timeline. It is highly probable that – if not in this life, then in at least some other lives associated with your soul – you are exploring reaching out for a substance or another person to fill a sense of emptiness. Some people will have understood from an early age or at some point realize or be told that they have what is called an "addictive personality" and this seems to explain the presence of these behaviors and tendencies to attempt to fill the inner emotional void with something or anything. If you relate to this description, I would like you to explore viewing this way that you are wired as part of your multilife soul journey to learn about becoming the source of love. Experiencing pain, as noted above, is a normal and necessary part of the human experience. Soul sets out to explore all avenues and possibilities of human experience and this includes pain. But the overall plan for the success of the manifestation experiment is that you learn to become the source of love. This means that at some point you will look up from being in the midst of your daily life and realize that there is not enough love in your life, that you feel empty and not driven to do much of anything because you do not feel loved or supported.

This is an intense topic for many. Some of you have become expert at judging yourself for what seem mistakes and missteps. If you are feeling not sure about taking all of this in because it might mean that there are more reasons to judge yourself, please take a deep breath and make the decision to give yourself the benefit of the doubt as a divine being learning how to live. While your true nature as All That Is is all-knowing, your human personality is not! You cannot be so, of course. No one is really expecting you to be perfect unless you are expecting it. So take a moment and decide to be easy on yourself so that you can read on and be able to be informed in positive ways about how all of this works. You deserve the benefit of learning more about this bigger-picture stuff and, as long as we're here together, let's stay open to letting the story continue to unfold. If you judge yourself or have a creeping sense that you perhaps should be judging yourself, the door to allowing this information to come in can close and that is the last thing that I want to happen for you.

And so what is it that gets in the way of a meaningful life? It is the experience of a lack of love, not being clear that meaning is only possibly found by you creating it, and not realizing that all that comes to you is a manifestation of your own energy field so that you-as-All That Is can learn about what it means and requires to live human life.

The need for meaning coexists with the distraction of your emotions, feelings, and thoughts about what happens now and what has happened to you in the past.

In one sense, it is your relationship to your emotions and your willingness to believe one narrative about why things have happened to you that gets in the way of creating meaning. Think about it this way: If you are distracted by your emotions, including your sense of being a victim, anything that is out of place in your feeling self, grudges, longings, and the like, you cannot manifest a life that reflects becoming the source of love. If living in this sort of distracted state, you will not have the space inside you to come from a place of love or even see that your motivation at times or often might be sourced in something other than love. Excess emotional elements – you might at times call them "baggage" – encumber you and prevent you from living a heart-centered life and thereby creating the meaning that you crave.

Another way to look at this is that if you perceive that you are not loved, your emotional world will be out of joint. If you perceive that others owe you or that you must wait for something loving and supportive to come to you before you can see your way to believe that it's possible, your emotional world will be imbalanced. The sense of needing something from others is prevalent in humans. While it is important for the long-term, multilife journey of soul living human lives in order to learn about what love is, etc., it is not your destination. *If you wait for someone to love you, then you live a life of waiting.* I cannot emphasize strongly enough that becoming the source of love for yourself is the remedy for all that ails you emotionally. Being the generator of love, incidentally, does not mean that others cannot or will not interact with you and love you. It simply means that you are not waiting for others in order to have love in your life. Becoming the source of love for yourself will have you surrounded by more love, in fact, because you are at that stage vibrating lovingly and therefore attracting love to you.

Along the way to becoming the source of love, you must love yourself in all the ways that others have not. Whether they didn't do something well enough or did something terribly – and each result can end up with you hurting – or were simply unavailable or couldn't see and validate you, they were functioning for you as triggers to learn more about the need to become the source of love for yourself. At the time you simply experienced pain, loneliness, abuse, neglect, or something else, and this is what you may feel now because it is imprinted upon your emotional body and tied up with the meaning you have given it. Can you rewrite your history to reflect that these experiences were designed by the souls involved – by portions of All That Is – to give you the opportunity to see more about what happens when you do not become the source of love for yourself? Remember that whatever you are vibrating in fact manifests the world around you. If you are vibrating, "I was/am not loved enough," then that is what you are in this moment creating around you. Decide to view all who have not loved you in the right ways, enough, or at the right times in terms of this teaching on soul and its long-term journey to learn about what love is, where it comes from, and who's responsible for giving it to whom.

When you make the decision to become the source of love, you will find a strength inside you that has always been aching to come out. It might seem a sense of determination mixed with relief that you can be loving to yourself and others in all the ways that you have not felt loved by others. Making this choice will free you to begin a process of ending entanglements you may have with others that are based in you and them trying to get something from each other that, in fact, each party needs to give to the self. Ever wondered why you have so many relationships of various kinds over the course of your human life? *It is to provide all involved numerous opportunities to fail to get from others what they perceive they need from others.* Through one lens, this is the natural, normal function of all human relationship!

How does that idea make you feel? What comes up for you when you read that? To be clear, I do not say this to ruin the idea of relationship for you but to provide you more information on what is actually happening in your dynamics with others than you usually have. If you feel a little bubble burst at the thought above, then you are experiencing what we might call "the death of romance," and this is a very positive thing. If you think that someone else can do something for you and you are trying to get it or waiting for it or asking for it – all of these things – then you are not becoming the source of love. If you are waiting for someone to save you from loneliness, unhappiness, or anything else, including yourself, you are not becoming the source of love. In those cases you are trying and waiting, and this is not empowering for you as a portion of All That Is learning to become the source of love for yourself. In fact, relationships with others serve to bring elements of yourself out so that you can learn about yourself as a human and as a loving being.[5]

Relationships are just one area of life but they figure prominently as humans learn about what love is, where it comes from, and who's responsible for giving it to whom. Consider that all of your relationships are manifestations of your energy field

---

[5] See the channeled book *Approaching Love* for a detailed exploration of this topic.

and, therefore, one category of all the creations you are vibrating into existence in the world around you in order for your soul to learn about living a human life.

Judgment, Shame, and Guilt

It is here that I wish to take a detour into a specific area of life experience and emotional quality of life that all humans experience to one degree or another. As we look at what gets in the way of living a meaningful life and intentionally creating your life as the source of love, know that judgment, shame, and guilt can figure prominently.

Some of you have become wired to measure yourself against external standards to such a degree that thinking about becoming the source of love while in human form can be truly perplexing. Being oriented to judge yourself against someone else or your work or effort against a preestablished benchmark is not abnormal. In fact, it is part of the long-term experience of All That Is to learn about what love is, where it comes from, and who's responsible for giving it to whom. Every human at some point needs to learn to validate the self – to be loving toward and accepting of the self – and perceiving that one has not measured up or made mistakes is part of the process.

Above I mentioned a bit about judgment and asked you to take a deep breath and accept that no one expects you to be perfect unless you are doing so. I wish to be clear that if your journey to learn about love includes overcoming self-judgment, it is a given that along the way, as you live human lives, you will draw others to you who judge you. You will magnetize into your life – whether through relationships or family dynamics – others whose expectations you cannot meet. All humans are wired to one degree or another to want to be liked because you need to be loved. Many spend lifetimes looking for the approval of others so that there exists at least some love. If you are someone who experiences self-judgment, shame, or guilt, this text as a whole is doubly important for you. This is because measuring the self against an external situation is an exercise in giving something else the power to define who you are.

That phrase might seem a bit out of place here so let me explain. When you look for validation or approval from another, you are putting in that person's or that situation's hands your ability to love yourself. In many ways your entire culture is based upon the goal of receiving support and encouragement from external sources. It is part of the process for All That Is to learn about receiving love versus generating it. It is therefore a creation of All That Is, and this means that it is normal for you and others to cycle through. Yet at some point along the way, something might have become extremely important to you, such as a desired experience or outcome. When this happens, it seems easy to put a great deal of energy in the direction of getting that desire or need met – having that experience or seeing that outcome come into existence. How much energy can you extend in the direction of getting something, of experiencing some form of outer approval and validation? You can, in fact, bank the integrity of your life force – your vitality and passion – on this thing or situation happening or not happening, depending upon your desire. And so it happens that sometimes along the way you do not get what you want and all that you banked on it can seem wasted and/or lost. It does not have to be gone from you if you understand the true purpose of opportunities that come to you – to teach you more about what love is, where it comes from, and who's responsible for giving it to whom – because then you can retain your sense of personal power no matter how particular scenarios turn out.

All of this is meant to paint a picture of humans who judge themselves for not measuring up or not delivering something as conceived or promised might find themselves consistently or even chronically oriented toward the external to show them that they deserve love. But since all of creation exists in order to show you in what ways you perceive you are not getting love from others and external sources, the universe does not rush in to validate you (unless you are drawing in codependent situations to your life to show you how to make the search for love worse before you can make it better by becoming the source of love). If you are waiting for external sources to validate you then you will live a life of waiting. It will not happen in a meaningful way that fills in the spaces left when others have not loved you the way that you needed and wanted.

These situations can lead to cycles that become downward spirals. Many times those who look for such validation – love and permission to be the self fully and without apology or regret – and do not find it end up in various ways hurting themselves. For some it is not long before the sense of emptiness can begin to lead to behaviors meant to fill the inner void, the sense of a lack of love. As the rest of this text describes, your ability to be spiritually and in all other ways healthy depends on your willingness to be the source of love for yourself. How long it takes you is entirely within your power. Ultimately all beings will get there because this is the point of the manifestation experiment we are all living out. If you are someone who relates to this sense of emptiness that has lead to self-destructive behaviors, please begin to view yourself not as someone who is doing something wrong or who deserves punishment for one reason or another, or perhaps for every reason. Choose now to view yourself as a work in progress, a divine being who has at times been clueless about how to be the source of love for yourself. You have not been taught this and so you have perhaps not seen how to do it. Maybe you know this but have perceived that you are not strong enough to make it happen. You are the only one judging yourself and you can at any time step into your divine power by learning to view your life as an outgrowth of your soul's intention to learn through becoming loving.

Your Defining Beliefs and How to Change Them

Now let us return to focus on existence of the narrative that you have developed that seems to tell you who you are, what life is about, and what love is – to name just a few things. Each human has one. It is a natural part of being who you are as long as your mind is allowed free reign to do what it pleases. Through this text and other materials I provide, I aim to reveal to you how all of these things in your life are working so that you can see how to make more informed choices. What your history, experiences, and feelings mean – what you have decided they mean – is a narrative that has been written by parts of you attempting to make sense of them. You have put yourself in a story in order to weave a sense of meaning out of what occurred and how it has felt.

At this point in your development over multiple lives, it is time for you to see this narrative of yours for what it is. You are ready to begin dismantling it in order to get on with what you-as-soul came here to do: To figure out more about what love is, where it comes from, and who's responsible for giving it to whom – become the source of love.

It is up to you to be willing to see this story for what it is. I want you to honor that parts of you have written it because they have done so as a setup to for you to be able to protect yourself later when circumstances that seem to portend the repeat of something painful take shape. The narrative you have written serves to spell out why things happened the way they did and why they happened in the order that they did. This functions to keep you aware of perceived cause-and-effect scenarios so that you can avoid pain later. Really, you are very clever! All peoples have done this throughout time through developing mythologies, stories they tell each other about how and why the world works and what is a person's place in it. Your personal mythology comprises a series of narratives that depict what has hurt you and why you perceive they have happened. They are meant to be used by future yous (you at older ages) to defend against threats and to protect against the hint of something unhappy that came to you in the past coming to you again.

As I mentioned above, most of your narratives were written by younger yous without access to the wisdom you have developed through years of life experience living as a human. Most of these stories you tell yourself about what happened to you that was painful and how and why it happened are based in, we could say, a young and inexperienced journalist's perspective. This young person doesn't necessarily have all the facts about what was happening and why but nevertheless creates a story about it in order to try to understand what happened why it happened. If you decide to go through your personal history – your own personal mythology made up of these narratives written by less-wise, younger yous – then you will find a marked and distinct lack of presence in their retelling. You will note that you are repeating the story almost as if by rote, a bit robotic – obviously memorized. If you are grounded and clear, you will also notice that none of the stories are told from a place of love. Think about that: Your personal mythology is comprised of narratives written in fear! If you are going to become the source of love now, you will need to be present with what is happening in front of you in the moment – you will need to be fully present and so these stories will have to go! Think about the stories you've told yourself about what has happened and why it has happened. Check the frequency that you begin emitting when the story begins or when you focus on the feeling. It is all about fear – it has nothing to do with being loving, open, generous, and kind or giving anyone or anything the benefit of the doubt.

And so if you think about the stories you tell yourself that have shaped you, you will become aware of some beliefs that have served to define you. At times you will need to learn to read between the lines in order to see the belief behind the story, and so I invite you to turn your cleverness to unraveling the stories that you carry about the difficult and painful situations of your life history. As explored above, each is in fact an opportunity for your human self to live out the mission of soul to find out how to become the source of love. Taking this into account, it will be easy for you to see the importance of rewriting the history of what has happened to factor in the logic of soul. If you do not rewrite the meanings ascribed to your experiences then you are regarding your divine creations and co-creations as the source of victimhood. *Victim-related states are based in and are nurtured by a sense of powerlessness and define one as powerless.* If you can stretch your conception of who you are to include your true nature as soul, then you put yourself in a position to view the already well-established fact that you have been creating your life all along. You have been all these things happen and, even better, there is a good reason that you-as-soul have done this.

When a person emits a frequency based in fear, several things happen. First, fear is vibrated into existence around him or her in the form of other people and situations that carry or inspire fear. Second, as the person operates according to a fear-based vibration, he or she begins to affect his or her energy level, self-esteem and self-confidence, emotional stability, and the physical body in negative ways. When a person becomes fearful, fear takes over and that wonderful sense of divine power through making self-interested choices in line with what you came to the planet to do is covered over, seemingly lost. For some it will appear to escape them even as they struggle to reach for it. They will not see that energies, attitudes, and beliefs from the past that are held on to are, in fact, interfering with their ability to generate something other than fear.

And so how are you to change these beliefs? Don't worry – I won't be telling you to simply change your mind and that's that. It's a bit more complicated but is certainly straightforward enough that all humans can do it if they so choose. Yes, you are to change your mind about details and particulars, but you are also to honor the fact that the harmful and negative (which is to say fear-based) attitudes, beliefs, and thoughts are in place because of something that has happened to you. I want you to honor the fact that you feel and even that you have carried pain forward from the past. Some people are taught to, or figure out on their own, how to judge themselves for feeling pain, for not just letting it go. As all humans are poised to learn at some point, strength as a human is not in shrugging off emotions and deciding that one is tough enough not to be hurt or, if hurt, tough enough to go on. You are wonderful as a species, but through your disconnect with the natural feminine you have adopted these sometimes macho ways of being that, simply put, do not serve you. Strength as a human comes from being willing to feel all one can and dealing effectively with what one feels now and has felt in the past. Living a heart-open and heart-centered life is necessary for real human strength to develop but it is not in spilling your heart out all over the floor every 10 minutes. It is in feeling and effectively working through what you feel both present and past.

If you do not honor the reality that you have been shaped by your experiences and that the impact of certain life events and your feelings about them can run deep, then you are not honoring your true nature as a portion of the divine. If you focus on your emotions and feelings and broadcast that you are a victim of what has happened to you, then you are similarly not honoring that true nature. So, please accept the reality that you are shaped by what has hurt you while you commit to owning all of it as your creation or cocreation, vibrated into existence so that you-as-soul, as All That Is, can learn about how to deal with such situations and the feelings that result from them and the choices one must make in response to them.

And so you are to choose to respect the fact that you have been thus shaped while you commit to learning to view those experiences as serving an important process. By taking ownership of your creation, you step to the edge of releasing others from the perception that they have hurt or wronged you. You step out of feeling the victim and step into the knowledge that these other souls-as-people have created dynamics with you that have enabled God and Goddess to learn what it comes to Earth to learn as humans.

Consider a painful experience in your past in which someone seemed to hurt you. Try on for size this perspective and see if you are ready to forgive that other person for your perception that he or she is some sort of villain. Decide in the moment to own what you have cocreated with that person and that you are willing to learn to see how it is a creation that serves your divine journey as a soul living life as a human. Do not own this and forgive that person because you think you probably deserve poor treatment and so that person can be let off the hook. View that person as a soul, an incredibly powerful divine being, in cahoots with you-as-soul to cocreate what each of you needs to learn. If you were hurt in that situation, then it was serving you to be hurt. If that person hurt you, then the experience of hurting another was part of the plan for that other soul. Always learn more about this. Always seek to understand more about how things work behind the scenes and what you are to learn from the various situations that come to you in your life.

Changing your defining beliefs happens through this process. You must go through your history and do this ownership and forgiveness process with all the people who have hurt you, whom you have hurt, those who perceive you owe them something, and all whom you perceive you owe. Clear things out and clean them up, always owning your experience as your creation and always doing so knowing that you-as-soul have not created painful experiences as a desire to or from a sense of deserving punishment but as a means to learn how to make choices and deal with the consequences, as well as how to learn to align your motivation with love.

If you are not yet sure what defining beliefs may be within you, check your fears. List what you fear most and then let those parts of you speak: What is the worst that can happen? What is the terrible thing that is coming? Why do I believe this? What am I afraid of more: the event or my response?

And then look at the patterns of your life. What kinds of relationships and responses (or lack of responses) from others have shaped you? What kinds of opportunities do you perceive, if any, escape you – and why do you believe they do? Who is in charge of your life? What gives them the power? What would you have to do get back your power?

These are just two avenues into uncovering potential patterns. All humans are run by their beliefs and so it becomes critical for each to become aware of what he or she believes and why. These beliefs are not limited to the religious or ideological kind, or even just the political. They have to do with what is happening in the world and around and to you and what it seems to mean. One example could be a person who does not ask others for what she wants. Perhaps as a child, a parent was at key moments unavailable to give her the attention she needed and when she asked, she was told, "Not now – another time." She could begin to consider that it might mean something about her that this happened. Maybe she wonders if she's not lovable or not worth the time. Or maybe she just comes to think that others are unavailable or uninterested in her. Over time this will shape her interactions with others and if we were to catch up with her in her 40s or 50s, the thought that she had as a child that became a belief we will see has been running a corner of her life. Chances are she will not see it as a belief but the way that things are. If she looks at the pattern in her life regarding her desires and, communicating them to others, she might list this one if it seems important or abnormal to her, relative to her perceptions of others' experiences. All of this is to say that viewing a pattern and your feelings about it will reveal much about the underlying belief of yours that creates it – what you might not even know to be a belief.

Death

Now that we have discussed life, let us move on to death and its relationship to life. Death is a part of life, as you know. Not only in that it is inevitable and inescapable for all living beings but also in that it is a punctuation point that inspires and shapes how you live. I mean that you know it will come but most of you do not know just how and when, and so the idea of it can inform how you live your life. Therefore, it is necessary to understand life as described and explored above in order to truly understand the role of death in relation to life.

The perspectives that I will share with you will cover a number of angles. You will read below about what happens at the moment of death from the perspective of human consciousness as well as from that of the soul. Also, you will read about the process that follows this moment and what is to happen during what we consider to be your orientation process to the afterlife. Before we get to that, however, I'd like to explore some issues surrounding death that might have come to inform your current conception of death and what comes after it.

The first thing to say is that your religions are mostly mistaken. They are attempts to explain death using the logic of the human mind and presumptions and beliefs about life, soul, deities, and the universe. They offer explanations of what someone thinks is happening or what they perceive that a deity has told them happens at and after death. But mostly these approaches are designed to cause you to live in a way that supports the religion's agenda so that you can support and maintain its existence. Essentially, religions are political organizations co-opting spiritual teachings and they need people to believe certain things so that the organization can receive resources from them and, ultimately, thrive and prosper. This is fine for what it is: An exercise for humans to attempt to find meaning and connection to the divine and, in the process, create institutions that can help them in various ways. But you are not through these sources going to get the straight story on death and what occurs after it. You are instead going to get a story that is geared toward inspiring you through either love or fear to support the political and economic agenda of one group or another. And all of this makes sense as you do not have many examples of people telling credible stories of dying and coming back to life. Those who have what are termed near-death experiences (NDEs) certainly have something to say about what they experienced. But without much corroboration from sources deemed rational in human terms and therefore worthy of taking seriously, it might not often be taken seriously. The people who run your religions can tell you that what this person is saying is not what God is saying and humans will tend to believe it because the new story – from the person who had the NDE – doesn't necessarily fit with and support what they have been told by those running the religions is true. I will discuss NDEs more below.

Some of you fear death. Others accept it as part of life. From your human perspective, it is the end for you. Of course, if we factor in what soul is and how life works on this planet related to the logic of soul, we know that this is not the case. From your human perspective a person is living and then a moment comes when something happens and the person is no longer living. That person is gone and he or she is gone forever. There is no negotiation. There is no hoping that death might not happen turns things around. It is a permanent state and now everyone still living must move on or figure out how to try to move on.

Death, therefore, appears to be the end of life. It is of course, in fact, the end of a particular, embodied life. But life goes on. Life continues. If you are willing to shift your frame of reference to that of soul, of All That Is endeavoring to learn about what it means to be human, then you are able to see that, as part of All That Is, when a person dies nothing but the body dies. This is not meant to rob the looming specter of death of meaning. But it is meant to rob the reality of the meaning that has arisen for you if it is something about hopelessness, futility, being overpowered, or anything else that makes you feel small and unimportant.

One of the vexing and confounding parts about life is the reason behind many kinds of deaths. You perceive there are accidental deaths and unwarranted, undeserved deaths. You have come to believe that death robs people of their potential if it comes to them on the cusp of a big opportunity or at an age you deem too young to have really lived.[6] To really get to the bottom of what death is and how it functions for soul and All That Is, you must shed any and all ideas you may have picked up and held onto that death in some way functions as a punishment for something done wrong or something not done. From the perspective of All That Is, of divine source, there are no just deaths as there are no unjust deaths. Births are the beginnings of life chapters and are chosen to provide the right kind of genetics and conditioning to the newly-erupting soul (erupting into the Earth dimension as a human) and all births are perfect as openings of life chapters.

The end of a particular life comes when the chapter of that life is complete from the perspective of soul. The soul has had the opportunity to view human life through the lens of a particular kind of personality with certain kinds of conditioning – and, therefore, certain kinds of beliefs, skills, knowledge, and feelings. Certain varieties of human experience possible only through the particular lens of that person's life have been observed, felt, and noted by soul. The work of that particular human

---

[6] See the channeled volume *Understanding Loss and Death* for more on this.

manifestation is complete and this is the only way that death can occur. Again, there are no accidental deaths. Deaths are the endings of life chapters and are chosen to wrap up one human story once that story has showed soul one route to living as a human given certain contextual meaning based in training, knowledge, feelings, and beliefs.

There is a deep well of issues surrounding death that many of you reading this will need to learn to understand and bring back into balance before the rest of this text will truly sit well with you. If you are carrying pain about past or recent deaths of others and the apparently senseless nature of them, then you might find what comes next objectionable. It is normal for humans not to be open to perspectives that challenge the beliefs that they are carrying and doubly so when those beliefs relate to or are caused by pain that is clouding things within them. When you are in pain, parts of you struggle to come up with reasons why you are feeling that way – perhaps about why it happened and what it means – because they are trying desperately to understand what is happening. No being likes to be in deep emotional pain and so reasons are sought to try to figure out where things went wrong and, possibly, how it can be fixed now by stepping back or changing some element of the story that lead one to this place of pain. But through the lens of pain, your sense of being able to think through, feel into, and sense the truth of things is impaired, and this is normal and natural. So it is that I invite you to be aware of what might come up for you as you continue reading this text and encounter all that it contains. It is meant to help you see new levels of what is going on surrounding death, and yet I understand that being in this space might bring up challenging emotions and thoughts within you.

Death and the Multilife Journey

It is important to note that when you are dealing with feelings, fears, thoughts, and beliefs about death, you are not simply doing so regarding this life. You are in fact dealing with feelings, etc., about death that might stretch across time. This means that you are now, as you live your life, potentially dealing with feelings about and memories of death that belong to other manifestations of your soul on different parts of the Earth timeline. In this present life of yours, you will at times have access to fears, feelings, and memories related to other lives of your soul on the timeline that have to do with death. For many, this becomes about the manner in which some other manifestation of their souls is dying on the Earth timeline. Intense fears and phobias in this life can be rooted in situations elsewhere on the timeline that lead to or threaten death. The things that you are most afraid of in this life may represent ways that other yous have died elsewhere on the timeline.

This can stretch the mind, surely. When one gets deeply into details of the process of living a human life that reflect how the emotional body connects all of a soul's manifestations together across the Earth timeline, it can boggle your linear, logical circuits to take in how it all works. For now, just get comfortable with the picture of your most serious fears being rooted in multiple places along the Earth timeline and that other-life deaths can inform your fears now.

If you are in touch with these fears and you let them have a voice in your world, you may carry a fear that seems to imply or point to death and may seem to mean that you are not safe. At first glance this can be tricky for a human to deal with. This is because if you are afraid of something, it will be drawn to you (as explored above regarding the logic of soul). When you become aware of deep fears and they persist, you can begin vibrating the fear into the world around you, emitting a broadcast signal that you are afraid. With enough of this signal broadcast, you will begin to draw scenarios to you that seem to confirm that you were right to be afraid. I suggest that when you are dealing with difficult emotions, you decide unequivocally that you are always safe. If you do not know that you are safe, then the fear can snowball within you and the signal broadcast can become louder and louder because there is no contrasting opinion. If you do not decide that you are safe, then the part of you that carries the fear can take over – there is no opposition. If the smart, sophisticated, and savvy part of you who finds and reads texts such as this one in order to learn and grow as a human and as a spiritual being is silent, then any old part of you carrying some fear from earlier in your life or from another spot on the Earth timeline (another life of your soul) can take over. I cannot emphasize strongly enough the importance of deciding that you are safe! It is so important, in fact, that it is what I tell all humans I interact with. When you call this channel and ask me a question through him I always tell you to get grounded and connected to the Earth and decide that you are safe. You have lived long enough on the Earth – over multiple lifetimes – in fear of death, that you have experienced all the possible outcomes that can result from carrying and losing yourself in fear.

The last thing you want to have happen is for fear to take over. But really what happens is that you cede control to fear because you do not know what to do with it. It is intense and can seem to take you over or threaten to do so. It rushes up from an unknown place and can fill you up. What is happening is that a part of you who carries a fear rushes to the surface of conscious awareness when something in your thoughts, feelings, and/or environment seems to point to something that this part of you carries fear concerning. For example, if you are afraid of water you might have another life during which you have a terrible experience almost drowning or in fact drowning. Now in this life, when you have perhaps had more or less an okay relationship with water, something might trigger you and this part or your emotional self can rush to the surface. You have been going about your business with a particular kind of "I am me" status quo and suddenly your sense of "I am me" balance is disturbed. You might feel unsure and shaky. You might not know how to continue with your previous rhythm because there is a new variable present – the fear of water, and often it will feel like death is around the corner so it is really a fear of death. I encourage you to develop a consistent grounding practice of connecting to the Earth and centering your consciousness's center of gravity in your body so that when a fear comes up, you are not so susceptible to being shaken off course by its sudden appearance.

When you know that you are safe, your relationship with and ability to work intentionally and consciously with fears that may come up from under your surface changes for the better. You are less shaken by something coming up. You will feel it, certainly, and it will affect you. But when grounded, you will know that it is temporary and you will know that you have the choice in how to deal with it. You will at this point be able to remain in your body and know that you are strong enough to deal with anything that comes up. If you do not know that you are safe, you cannot possibly decide that you are strong. So please get grounded, decide that you are safe, and know that you are strong. You are, after all, a portion of All That Is, and All That Is is definitely strong!

Some of you might wonder why you have to deal with fears that do not belong to you – your personality and human "I am me" identity. This is part of the process of becoming conscious of your multidimensional nature, meaning that you are in fact more than your personality and conditioning and you exist across time as consciousness, energy, and emotion. Allowing this into your awareness and intellectually observing it as a phrase and possibly true is not enough. You must learn to deal with the energies and emotions that your soul has set out for you to learn about. Is it really unfair that you have to deal with these fears from other humans at different points along the Earth timeline? If you think you are your human self, then you may be hard-pressed to accept the invitation to do so. If, however, you are willing to adapt to the truth that you are more than this particular personality you carry and set of conditioning scenarios that have shaped you in this life, then it becomes easier. Your mind will at times be stretched if you accept this invitation from your soul, and life will undoubtedly become richer and more fulfilling as you learn to see all that has happened to you and all that happens to you now as cocreations of divine beings each trying to figure out how to become the source of love by cycling through fear and observing and dealing with the results.

Make the decision now to be grounded the next time that a deep fear of yours surfaces. Most of them that you carry will have been with you a long time. It is, in fact, rare that an event happens in mid- or late-life that triggers a fear associated with another life of your soul lived elsewhere on the timeline. You will have had many opportunities to become aware of your deepest fears early in life when you are unwittingly vibrating your experiences into existence around you. They can intensify as you age because, as described above, the power of fear can grow if the parts of us carrying the fear – those that are unresolved about feeling safe, strong, and powerful – are allowed to take over. If you lose your sense of who you are, then you cannot possibly access the sense of strength that comes from knowing that you are additionally a wise portion of All That Is trying to remember your wisdom through a long process of learning about what love is, where it comes from, and who's responsible for giving it to whom.

Some of these deepest fears will, as stated above, be about how other yous elsewhere on the timeline have died or come close to death. They can have such a power over you that you may avoid getting anywhere near scenarios and circumstances that contain elements of what did lead or seemed to lead to that death. With the example of drowning in another life, you might in this life avoid being subject to bodies of water. You might not have any issue with a shower or a bath but being next to a lake, river, or ocean might make you squirm. Viewed in this way, it is obvious and understandable that a person would avoid being subject to bodies of water in which he or she might not have or might lose control over the self. The self and others can view this fear as irrational and in need of letting go, but this makes no difference when the fear comes up if it takes the person over. Somewhere on the Earth timeline a person associated with this soul – and sharing the same emotional body – is experiencing something terrible, out of control, and/or defeating around or in a body of water. *The feelings coming up in the person are real – the potential, terrible reality feels in fact real to that person because it is happening somewhere else on the timeline. It feels real because, to the emotional body, it is.* Soul knows no time and the emotional body as it is shared by all lives associated with that soul is not operating merely on one or another part of the timeline but in all of them. It is all happening simultaneously – both the manifestations of the soul's chosen themes and the emotional imprints that result from real-world human experience to teach soul about those themes. The person feels it because it is being felt by another human associated with his or her soul somewhere else on the timeline.

And so you need to know generally that you carry such fears about something or other. Probably you carry several such fears. Know that you have triggers and that parts of you – pieces of personality from other humans associated with your soul, people living elsewhere on the Earth timeline – will rise to the surface and assert themselves through the imprint they took on when something tragic and terrible happened that lead to their deaths or scared them so deeply that they thought death was at hand. It is safe to assume that over the course of many thousands of lives, you will have had the opportunity as a human to die in just about all possible ways. It is safe to assume that you have died in natural disasters – volcano eruptions/lava flows, earthquakes, tornadoes, tsunamis, etc. You have surely died in war, whether a combatant or not. You have probably been murdered with intent at times and also at other times accidentally. You have undoubtedly starved. It is entirely probable that you have taken a risk athletically, sexually, politically, and/or in some other way that resulted in death. The same with burning in a fire or at the hands of others, eating poisonous plants by accident or being poisoned, having your homeland invaded and raided, suicide, being tortured to death, and just about anything else you can imagine, including heavy things falling on you. Oh, and I didn't even mention animal attacks and stampedes or a thousand other things. Varieties of deaths are myriad, and across the timeline your soul's other lives are sampling a great many of them.

Whatever triggers for you that might exist all across the timeline will not all show up at once. You as a particular human are going to be dealing during your life with a certain set of these deep fears and, usually, one by one. This is to say that all of your soul's other lives will not bleed through into your consciousness all the time. What does enter your awareness (often through these fears we are discussing) is determined by what in your field is most in need of resolution. It is not your natural state to remain in tension, and so unresolved issues will come to the surface of conscious awareness so that you have the chance to resolve them one way or another. When it comes to all these ways of dying all over the Earth timeline, what you will remember most and most frequently through these fears will be those that resonate with the particular conditioning scenarios you have had in this particular life.

What needs to be resolved in your life in this way might be attributable to intentions you have set for yourself. For instance, if you feel bored in your life and decide to set up some adventures for yourself, it could be that an adventure-seeking other life of your soul's in which something painful or tragic happened might come to the surface. Imagine deciding to take a trip to some far-off locale you've never visited and do things that you've never done before. You might get a book or brochure or look up photos online and see some improbable bridge spanning an impossible chasm and start to choke up with fear and trepidation. It could be that you were surprised at the image but it could also be that another life associated with your soul that died somehow in a way related to such a bridge or such a chasm is asserting itself, being triggered by the implication that he or she would have to again go through that death and all that was felt in association with it.

Think about what it looks like to someone who is not you who might witness this. This other person will have his or her own triggers but perhaps not the ones you have. He or she might try to help you in essence come back to reason but it can be hard for you to do so. You are reacting emotionally to the threat of a repeat of a terrible thing another you has experienced in his or her life.

Consider all the ways that people die and how many people are alive on the Earth. There is such an incredible variety of multilife experiences surrounding death that generates an equally incredible variety of fear. And all of it is meant to teach you about becoming the source of love now – in any given moment, at all times.

Death as a Teacher and Near-Death Experiences

Now I would like to spend a moment discussing near-death experiences (NDEs). Many who have them report later to have seen a white light, to have heard a loving voice saying something or other, or a divine presence reflecting something or carrying a message of love or hope. These people can return to life and share what is meant to be an inspirational message but it doesn't mean that others are ready to hear it. They have seen, felt, and experienced something that has changed them and, often, cannot be articulated adequately because feeling surrounded by total and utter love – something that can happen when one encounters what is called "the light" – is not something easily communicated through human language. So it is that sometimes people who have this experience find others not receptive to the message they perceive they now have to share. This is part of the experience of seeing something many others have not seen and trying to communicate a truth one feels inherently to be true, which is a life theme that might be chosen by a soul for a human to live out and through.

From the perspective of soul what is happening with an NDE can be a wake-up call for this person to decide he or she wants to live. It could also be that in that state is the only way the guidance team can get through to the person – stopping the person in his or her tracks in order to communicate something necessary to his or her life path. Sometimes an NDE serves to inspire a person to cease destructive behaviors in order to sort through emotional debris that has clogged the life and made it difficult for the person to know and love the self. And sometimes an NDE can function to give a person a glimpse of the loving energy that can await one after death so that person can choose to live in a different way. Very often these are meant to shake a person out of a particular rhythm or put him or her on a new path for a positive, life-affirming reason.

Most of you will look at the fact that this person did die or almost died. From the soul's perspective – from the point of view of All That Is – there is no chance here, nothing random. If the person lived then there was no possibility that the person was going to die. You must learn to view all that happens to you and others as reflections of the power of the intentions of All That Is, creator consciousness, God and Goddess, et al. There are no accidents. You might view someone surviving an NDE as having experienced a miracle but you are invited to view all things as perfect, as fitting in with the plan that is the manifestation experiment you are all living as humans on Earth in the time-space dimension. Just as there are no accidental births, no accidental deaths, no accidental marriages or divorces, there are no accidental NDEs. All of these and other life events serve as vehicles for soul-as-humans to learn about what love is, where it comes from, and who's responsible for giving it to whom.

To extend this idea, consider how you have felt when someone you love is near death. Do you feel fear that this person will die? It is of course natural as a human to feel many things, including this. But I am asking you to explore also viewing what is happening as part of the soul's plan – the plan of All That Is – as it relates to the chapter of life that is this loved one of yours. Use memories of these experiences and your feelings about them to show you more about your human conception of what is happening here on Earth with all this living and dying. I invite you to be willing to feel all that you can feel so that you can become conscious of the overt and subtle dynamics that inform such situations. For example, when in the past a loved one of yours was near death, consider what you felt. Look at what you felt as a necessary part of All That Is learning about how important loved ones are or can be to a person. Consider that these are the times during which you will be reminded of human mortality and, therefore, the sense of meaning that you and others might not be creating in life. Perhaps mundane priorities have distracted you from creating a sense of meaning by giving to others and the world what you truly crave to give. A loved one near death can serve to inspire you to reprioritize and shift perspective in order to reconnect with what is most important to you, what you want to experience in life, and what you have to offer and give others and the world around you.

Whether related to your own or another's NDE or someone you love headed toward the inevitability of death, death is a teacher to show you more about your relationship to life. It is a crucial part of a portion of All That Is learning how to be human. Have you heard that funerals are for the living? This is the idea. Marking a death and remembering a person, perhaps celebrating his or her life, is an important part of the life process for all of you. You love others and form connections of various kinds. You create a life with them and they with you. Your energies and emotions are mixed up together – you love each other – so that all of you can learn in your own individual ways more and more about becoming the source of love for yourself. All of you are teachers for each other about what love is, where it comes from, and who's responsible for giving it to whom. Each and every single one of you affects others along such a path! It is really remarkable and beautiful when you look at it this way.

Giving and Taking Back Energy After a Death

It is important for you to learn about yourself as energetic beings. You cannot operate your human and divine self consciously if you do not understand how your energy field functions and how your emotions are related to it. For our purposes here I will share with you some necessary basics so that you can apply them to situations in your life relating to death and to a healthy grieving process that allows you to take in the full meaning of life and death when death occurs around you. I want you to be able to breathe in the enormity of the importance of life and make the most of it so that you can gracefully accept the inevitability of death and learn to appropriately grieve when it happens around you.

In the process of forming loving bonds with others, all humans share and exchange energies. Energy is felt by humans as emotion and when one person opens energetically to another in one kind of relationship or another, emotions flow. In each person, certain feelings are activated. In all important relationships between humans, certain places within the self are opening through the activation of feelings – when energies in others are met and encountered – and so emotional histories and landscapes are often brought to the surface in each person. Surely you have noticed that when a relationship begins there is a sense of newness – being activated by each other and brought more alive and in ways other than have been habitual – and then after a time things get harder. Each person brings to a relationship his or her emotional history and energetic imprints of having been bonded with others. Maybe at times it is annoying to you that old, unresolved family issues can come up in your partner-type relationships but this is the normal way that human emotional living works. You are are landscapes of inner emotional imprints gained from various relationships that have served in many different ways to teach you to become the source of love for yourself – to love yourself in all the ways that you have not been or felt loved by others. Other people always show you how you are not loving yourself or not filling in the gaps from your history of learning about love, where it comes from, and who's responsible for giving it to whom. But just because they reveal these dynamics within you to you does not mean that you automatically take them up on the opportunity! It is easy to see other people as the problems in your world, as bringing things up that you would rather not deal with – as though others can do anything without your energetic vibration manifesting it in front of you.

And so it is that humans carry into new relationships unresolved issues from their past. I mean to paint this picture for you as normal given how you have conceived of love and tried through your human personalities to love each other in the ways that you need and, perhaps, attempt to fill in gaps for each other when it comes to not feeling loved in the past. But I want to be completely clear that it is not a way of being in relationship that honors your true nature as a soul, a portion of All That Is striving to remember through this human life process your true nature as the source of love. It is part of the process and yet you are meant to move through it. All that has come before for you – the entirety of your biography when it comes to loving and not loving, feeling loved and not feeling loved – I invite you to accept calmly as part of the learning process for All That Is in human form that has forgotten its true nature. All that seems to you wasted or lost regarding your history of being loving, etc., should be viewed as part of the multilife learning curve meant to connect you in time to your true purpose here on Earth, which is to become the source of love for yourself.

This is an immense topic, to be sure. For our purposes here I would like for you to understand that until you learn the difference, many of you live your lives carrying energies for others and having them carry energies on your behalf. These situations have arisen because you have loved each other or tried to do so. Energetic sharing that can become entanglement, in fact, reflects that you activate each other's deeper places as energetic beings, as emotional beings. You should take this to mean that as souls-being-humans you are interfacing and interfering with each other in loving ways in order that all souls have myriad opportunities to learn about the true nature of love and your own true nature as the source of it. Your day-to-day experience may be that someone who will no longer interact with you is on your mind often. It might also be that you have not said something important to someone from your past and you might not know how to broach the subject now even if you have contact with that person regularly. It could instead happen that you simply do not understand why a relationship ended the way that it did and want resolution. Each of these situations can indicate that there are still energies shared between you – that you have some energy from that other person and that person has some energy from you.

In the normal course of relationship it is important to gently give back all that you have borrowed from or are carrying on behalf of another and that you call back all energies you may have loaned or given to another. To be clear, to have the right kinds of relationships in your present, you must go through this process with all who have been part of your past whom you have loved and/or who have loved you.[7] But when it comes to death, it is even more important to go through this process of giving and taking back energy.

From your human perspective – that of your linear, logical mind – the opportunity is over. The person has died and that's that. He or she is gone. You are left, so to speak, holding the bag of the unresolved stuff that unfolded between you that one or both of you might have tried after the relationship

---

[7] See the channeled home-study course *Release: A Course for Healing* at tdjacobs.com.

was over to work through. But now, your mind says, it is over. The chances to resolve things seem gone.

In fact, it is entirely possible to do this after someone dies. You need to grieve the death of a loved one and this is right and good. Let this taking and giving back energy be part of your grieving process. It in no way meant to invalidate anything about the relationship. It is meant to allow each person to recognize the importance of the relationship so each can learn about the true nature of love and in what ways each might not love the self in the ways that are called for during his or her human journey. All of this has occurred because the souls involved chose to come together during life as humans on Earth in order to explore what love is, where it comes from, and who's responsible for giving it to whom. Each and every one of you has as a soul opted to interfere with others in order to reflect and show the others about what love is, etc. All humans are in this multilife process of bumping into each other and becoming entangled in sometimes confusing, painful, and tragic ways in order for All That Is to learn this critical thing it portions itself off and incarnates in order to learn as you and all the people you know. There is divine love driving all of your relationships, whether they are manifest on the human plane as celebratory or abusive. There is love behind all that happens to you and it is the love of the divine, of All That Is seeking to learn to love itself and remember while in human form how to become the source of love for one's self.

No one can move on following the death of a loved one, whether from the distant past or someone with whom one was involved up until death, without going through this process of giving and taking back energy. And so death can also function to show the surviving humans how to become whole again, how to develop healthy, clean, and clear energetic and emotional boundaries by acknowledging the importance of a relationship while also acknowledging that the self is still intact. Death is a teacher for an individual as it can reveal in what ways he or she has loaned out or forfeited his or her energies to another person. When such energies are exchanged it is done from a place of love and yet eventually, in time, one of the people is going to leave and/or die. One of the people in the relationship will be left to go on on his or her own. This is the normal and natural course of human relationships. This points to the fact that while your human selves can find it easy to believe that your relationships are meant to make you feel loved – and, therefore, you can feel loved as long that person is around and loving you – *but in fact your relationships actually serve to reveal to you more about your own process of learning to become the source of love for yourself.*

I want you to explore in your heart how you conceive of love. What is its purpose? What is the love of another person worth? What is the love of yourself for you worth? I want you to spend some time with these questions and others they may imply or call up and to do so while giving yourself the benefit of the doubt that you are a work in progress, that you are a soul not yet fully remembering your nature as All That Is and learning through trial-and-error what it means to be human and, in time, love yourself in all the ways that you need. I want you to free some time to sit with these questions and what feelings might arise when you encounter them and sip or chew on them slowly. I want you to journal about the inner dialogue that results. This is a good time to put down the text for a few days or a week or two as you explore what relationships are and have meant for you. Reading the rest of this text might be more comfortable after you've met some of the parts of self that you carry with you who have been shaped by what others do for, give to, and mean to you. If you want to continue, then by all means do. I simply want to point out to you that many humans will at this point in the text need to process something important that will have been trying to come to the surface to be resolved.

The Moment of Death

And now for the section that has drawn many of you to this text. Humans are intensely curious about the moment of death because it represents a mystery and, in fact, the final mystery. You have wondered for millennia if someone loving is there to greet you and you have feared that someone judging will be waiting for you in order to punish you. Depending upon what you believe will or might happen, you have shaped your living in order to live toward that kind of end.

Sometimes when people describe their NDEs they sound poetic and it can be hard to take in what they say. At times writers, thinkers, artists, and theologians have allowed their imaginations to run free as they picture pearly gates and harp-playing angels, a happy or unhappy bearded male god sitting on a throne in some way handing out gold stars or demerits. One of the things to know about the moment of death is that the human context is no longer applicable. Consciousness shifts out of the body. Your whole life, your sense of who you are has been tied to your body and, unless you have had numinous, mystical, or altered-consciousness experiences that have changed your idea of who you are, your life has likely been limited to a sense of being in your body. As it turns out, many people believe they are their bodies and the moment of death is a surprise because consciousness continues as it separates from the body.

For some, an explosion of the preexisting context of consciousness occurs, snapping their attention to what it is to be an energetic being. There can be a rush as awareness begins to be sensed outside the confines of the body and the previously-assumed limits of selfhood if the body was believed to be the self. For others, a gentle giving-way of what has always been (for the human) unfolds.

People nearing death often report seeing a light or witnessing a veil part. The boundaries between dimensions are ready to dissolve if the person is willing to see something new. Those who allow this to happen will become aware of the guides, masters, and/or angels that are awaiting the person's death. Each human has a guidance team made up of different sorts of beings and all of them are available to you. Most humans do not know this. Others have a sense of it or have heard directly and voluminously about it but might not believe that they deserve loving guidance and support. For others, such a team of disembodied beings might seem like enemies if he or she lived life trying to block out the existence of what cannot be seen but could not be ignored with the senses and emotions. You see, it is not uncommon for a person to believe that his or her mind is all there is. Humans are clever and over time usually become more so. The dominant cultural ethos on Earth for quite some time has had the primacy of mind and intellect – reason – emphasized above all else. Many aspects of your lives reflect this cultural value. At the moment of death the context of the self needs to change drastically and a newly-departed consciousness might not be willing to see what is there. If it is not open to the possibilities, it can create a sense of being closed and therefore what is in front of the consciousness can in fact not be loving. The loving frequencies that in fact await all who pass away are there but if one is not open, they will not be apparent.

This is how it is true that a person's predeceased relatives can be waiting to welcome him or her but the he or she cannot see them. The person might even wander around the time-space dimension, unsure how to transition into the next phase or not knowing that there is one. You have all heard of such spirits wandering around and your entertainment media have made much of turning these unfortunate situations into box-office smashes by frightening you about the unknown. They have no idea how it works, by the way, so you can go ahead and lose all the ideas that were scared into you through movies and television about tortured souls and ghouls that haunt people and try to hurt them. It is all nonsense.

If the newly-departed consciousness allows awareness of the guidance team much release and warmth can follow. Deceased relatives – those who died before the individual and have gone through what we call the orientation process – are there and have much to share with the individual consciousness. Now, in principle, this is soul itself but covered over by elements of personality that shape who the consciousness – the recently-dead person – thinks he or she is. Deeper elements of conditioning persist as do elements of personality such as opinions and certain kinds of emotional memories. I will explain what happens with these elements of self in the next section. Now I want to make clear to you that a recently-deceased individual whose consciousness has separated from the human body has a choice:

1. It can open to a new phase of identifying consciously as more than a person with a body and have its awareness stretched open to feel new vibrations of love and support, paving the way for the orientation process through which it will learn the purpose and function of all important relationships and choices during the recent human life, or

2. It can decide to remain closed to the unknown and not let anything new in, setting up what can be a lonely and painful process of wondering if there is safe haven and if anyone loves it, if it deserves to go to a good place but fearing that maybe there is no such place and no support.

What Happens After Death

Given the two possibilities listed above, there are two different ways that the post-death experience unfolds. Let's separate out each for you during this section and explain what each path holds.

Those Who Are Open to Receive Love

For those who are open to change and willing to drastically change in the face of the loving vibration that meets them, a process referred to as orientation begins to unfold. This contains a sort of schooling to teach this portion of consciousness that still retains elements of personality about all of his or her major life choices, important relationships, and life-shaping experiences. This is a transition time for the element of the soul that carries and needs to process elements of personality. Soul itself does not need this time but the human role the soul has been living through needs to be, so to speak, cleaned and calibrated. The emotional body has been further imprinted by this life and a debrief of sorts needs to unfold to bring all the facets of that particular human life into focus. The guidance team, including often relatives who have predeceased the individual, teach him or her to adapt the lens and filter through which his or her human self saw life, the world, the self, and others.

The goal of this orientation process is to help this personality-flavored aspect of soul turn all grievances and regrets into accepted pieces of the human learning journey for which he or she can be grateful to all the other souls involved in various situations and relationships for helping the soul-as-human to learn along its human journey. Views different from the human personality's are offered to the individual about how and why things happened during his or her life. It is about being oriented toward being loving, toward accepting love and understanding all that has happened to the person during life as part of the divine process of learning to become loving.

The process of coming out of judgment of self and other occurs outside the time-space dimension. Mostly these individuals in the process of orientation stay where they are but sometimes they can come back briefly and make contact with the living. Numerous living humans have had the experience of a loved one who has died coming back as a spirit to visit but there is something important that is different about the spirit of which the living human is very aware. There are many different reasons that this happens. All of the reasons have to do with nurturing the end or resolution of the relationship after death, including letting the living human know that the late loved one is okay, safe, happy, etc., or isn't judging the living human for anything and loves him or her. There is no rule about how often the late individual can visit a living loved one, by the way. When I say that they are in school, understand that it is not like any school you've been to! No one's watching the halls and making these beings watch and honor someone's clock-related behavioral code.

On that note, the orientation process takes different amounts of time according to Earth time for different beings. Sometimes the process unfolds quickly and sometimes it takes a bit longer. For instance, one person might have two parents who pass away in a short span of time and the mother seems to take years to go through orientation while the father passes through it rather quickly or the other way around. There are no rules and there are no expectations. As long as it takes for a recently-departed consciousness to process and learn is as long as it takes. Sometimes there are also variables to do with what is unresolved from the perspective of surviving loved ones. It could be that certain misunderstandings generated during the time when the two loved ones were both alive take time for the surviving human to unravel, forgive, and let go after the other person dies. It may be during this time that the surviving human experiences many synchronicities that remind him or her of the deceased loved one and the situation that was left unresolved. The deceased spirit can be making attempts to get through to the living loved one in order to show him or her that there is no grudge and no hard feelings. Remember that as the orientation process unfolds, the dead are learning about why they made the choices they did and what purpose those choices served in their lives and in the lives of those they loved and affected. Desertions, abuse, rapes, screaming, abandonment, betrayal, and other awful things are part and parcel of the human experience learning about what love is, where it comes from, and who's responsible for giving it to whom. Though painful for the people involved on both sides of the dynamics, they are necessary for All That Is to learn about becoming the source of love – learning to love the self in all the ways that others could, would, and did not love them. The dead during orientation can become oriented toward love (the entire point of the orientation process) and want to make contact with the living loved ones to let them know everything's okay, they are sorry, or they now can see the big picture and want the living loved one to know that this is so. It can be confusing to the living loved one who is trying to process his or her own feelings in one way or another (or trying to avoid them) and the dead loved one coming through might not be welcome. The synchronicities that bring the dead loved one into the living one's awareness on a regular basis might be dreaded and hated if the living person is not feeling loving and accepting. Remember that the surviving loved one is not going through the same orientation process! These synchronicities might, in fact, inspire anger toward the dead loved one, making the door to resolution impossible to open until the living person can get over the negative feelings and anger that is sourced deep under the surface in pain about the state or lack of resolution of the relationship.

Many true and heartfelt things go unsaid by humans to their loved ones during life for all kinds of reasons. Many of them have to do with judgment of self that is manifested as judgments of others, misunderstandings of all kinds, and a lack of willingness to apologize or be vulnerable enough to get to the bottom of deep emotional dynamics, including shared pain. It can happen that a deceased spirit wants to check in with living loved ones during the orientation process to make sure no one worries and to let them know that things are going according to plan.

Once the orientation process is complete, the newly-departed consciousness understands the choices, dynamics, and relationships of its human life. All of the choices made from fear are understood and peace has come into the individual's sense of self. It is clear to this being that the particular human life just completed served as a chapter in a long-term, multilife journey of a soul to learn about what love is, and it is at this stage that the individual is as close as possible to the loving nature of the soul itself. This is possible because the opinions, judgments, grudges, and regrets belonging to the human personality have been transformed through loving reflection into elements accepted by the individual as part of the journey of soul – of All That Is – to learn about what love is, where it comes from, and who is responsible for giving it to whom. At this point, if the departed spirit visits human loved ones, it will seem as if the being is lighter, wiser, and very different to deal with than the human person always was. Certain elements of self that identified the person when living remain but all the judgments, etc., are gone. Also the spirit can present the self to living loved ones appearing however he or she wants. Often they come through to those they are connected to in a young and healthy form, looking good and feeling even better. It is their option how they present themselves and is not about misrepresentation or to fool the living but about choosing how they want to be seen by living loved ones. Often the form chosen reflects the sense that everything is fine and that the departed person is doing well and the living need not worry about him or her.

It is at this stage that if it has been agreed to by all the souls involved, then the departed can function as a spirit guide for a living person. Not every deceased loved one becomes a guide after death but many do at least for a time. Often this occurs within families such that an older relative who passes away comes back after orientation to help out a surviving family member whom he or she knew while living. But it can also happen that members of previous generations of the family can serve as guides for a person. Another common scenario is that a person who has died and gone through orientation comes back to the Earth plane to be a guide for a person to whom he or she was not related during the most recent life. Your souls create nexi of loving, supportive connection across the vast expanse of the Earth timeline, and all souls are willing to receive loving, supportive guidance from anyone who will help out. It would not be out of the ordinary for you to learn that one of your guides now is a family member from one of your previous lives but was not related to you genetically in its most recent life or anyone that you in your present life have known. All portions of All That Is – all these souls – treat each other with loving kindness and want all the others to learn along their human journeys in the best possible way, and this is one way that they help make this happen.

Those Who Are Not Open to Receive Love

For the other group of newly-departed consciousnesses – those who are not open to change or fear they will not be loved and so cannot see it when it comes to them – it is, of course, a different story. They very often feel alone and this becomes a deep sense of loneliness. They might reach out to living humans so they don't feel so alone. In the process they may alienate the living because their vibration is one of fear and humans can discern this even if they don't have words to describe it. When approached with fear in any form, most humans are afraid or defensive in response and usually without thinking. When this happens with departed spirits who are wandering around, it can turn out negative for all involved. Very often the dead are looking for comfort, acceptance, and to know they are not alone but if they inspire fear in the living then they rarely get it.

It is possible for members of this group to change their minds at any time and open to receiving love. One of the functions of human psychic mediums can be to educate the dead who have not entered the orientation process about their options. These dead need to open to being loved and a living medium can get through to them and teach them to let go of what they have been holding onto that keeps them from opening to receiving love. Very often this fits into one of a handful of categories:

1. Judgments of their choices during human life.
2. Judgments real or perceived taken on about themselves from others.

3. Expectations that what is waiting for them – usually God – is not loving and accepting but will judge them for their human-life choices and flaws.
4. Perceiving a need to control the outcome of a time-space dimension event or decision (being unwilling to let go of worldly outcomes).

Often these people lived lives full of judgment of self and other. All criticisms of others indicates judging of the self and so it becomes that much more important, as a human, to become willing to open to becoming the source of love in your life. If you can traffic in love and give the benefit of the doubt to yourself and others that all are works in progress – and sometimes people make choices that seem unwise but trusting that these ultimately serve the learning journey of your soul – you are far better off when you die and are faced with the opportunity to see in what ways you might not be loving. For this is what happens when the newly-departed individual separates from his or her body: A louder, powerful, and very intense sense of love than most people encounter while living greets them. If a human has experienced it, it will have stopped the person in his or her tracks and caused a deeply emotional response.

Encountering this level of loving energy can inspire what you have heard described as fear and trembling – a deep sense of awe that changes one's life.

If you are aware of departed individuals who have not yet entered orientation, see if you can take some time to help them see the value of being loving toward themselves. This will open the door to being willing to receive love from others, including their guidance team and previously departed loved ones, those who will welcome them to what is often call "the light" once they are ready to go. In the long run it is not natural and normal for departed souls to hang around the Earth dimension and there are humans who, in their own process of learning about becoming the source of love, will perform the wonderful and kind service of helping these spirits cross over. So while it is not natural for it to persist, it is in fact a necessary part of the long-term, multilife journey of learning about becoming the source of love for the self. Even after death an individual can resist trafficking in love and being loving!

Think about someone you know in whom you find wonderful qualities that he or she cannot see. You want the best for this person and you wish that he or she could see just how great he or she is.

Sometimes you can do something to inspire this person to change his or her mind about the self but sometimes you cannot. Sometimes the person's beliefs are too strongly held to let your kindness and encouragement in. It is the same with these departed spirits who are not yet open to receive love.

The channel has done a fair amount of what is called spirit rescue and release, the process of helping souls do what is commonly called crossing over but we are here calling *entering orientation*. What he does is embody a sense of being loving and then recognize the departed for who he or she is – a divine being learning along a multilife process of learning to be loving. He explains through his heart that he or she can choose to let go of those opinions and judgments at any time. Embodying love and with no pressure, he is able to show them what's happening and what can happen next if he or she is ready and willing. Even if the departed spirit is not ready to leave yet, he or she is always able to understand the big picture the channel describes. Sometimes a living human is the only kind of being that can get through to them if they are not aware of or do not want to open to other kinds of beings, even if the other beings would surely welcome them as their guidance most definitely wants to do. The newly-departed consciousness must operate according to its own free will but it is important that it become informed about just what is going on and what their options might be.

When you consider such departed beings in the position of not knowing that they deserve and can open to receive love, look upon them with compassion. Understand that it is part of their human journey over the course of many lives to learn to become loving and that even after death some of you are not quite open to it. You may encounter one or more once in a while and feel fear – see if you can choose to generate love in the face of that fear. You would be doing a service to All That Is that, in fact, helps you, too, as that choice is part of your own process along the exact same journey.

Conscious Living, Conscious Dying

Given all that I have explained above about life and death, I now wish to shift focus to put your attention on how you can live in ways that prepare you consciously for death. It is not my desire that you begin to think about death and its inevitability on a regular basis or in any way obsess over it. By living your life now in open, full ways you can create the sense of meaning that all humans crave, thereby learning more about becoming the source of love. The point of all this is to nudge you toward living now, in other words.

It is a certainty that death will come to you but there are many variables that will determine what you let this mean and how you allow the fact of death to shape how you live your life. It is my intention as part of All That Is outside the game space of life to provide you with information and tools to help you navigate your choices yourself. All that I will offer in this section of the text is offered in the spirit that you might be able to see how to piece together a new sense of who you really are, what you came here to do, and how to make it happen even though the reality is that you will not live as this particular human self forever.

It is up to you if you want to make the reality of your eventual death rob you of the impetus to do create meaning with and out of your life. You are free to do whatever you please and this element of free will is an important ingredient in the All-That-Is playbook unfolding as you live your human lives all across the timeline. It is up to you to decide if you will embrace the time that you have and choose to deal in self-aware, conscious ways with what comes to you and what comes up within you along the way. As an energetic being experiencing life emotionally and a powerful creator manifesting in the world around you events and dynamics to reveal to you your hidden beliefs, it is as it happens inevitable that you will at times in life create and cocreate scenarios that confuse and hurt you.

Preparing for Death by Living a Meaningful Life Now

When you read the phrase, "preparing for death," you might think of the days or moments leading up to the end of a particular life. When it comes, you finally must face the reality of what will happen to you – that you will die – and you must somehow steel yourself to deal with the enormity of the feelings and the implications of what it means (usually that you didn't during life do something you meant, wanted, or needed to do). There is no escape – this is it. You must in this pressure-filled time decide how you will feel about what is happening, and certain parts of you find themselves in the position of needing to snap to attention and figure out if anything can be done to make things better or stretch them out longer.

Instead of your idea of that time and all that might go with it, I mean to put your attention on how you are living now as a preparation for death. If you choose to view death and the unknown with fear then you will find this notion uncomfortable. If, on the other hand, you are willing to adapt to a view of life and death as related to chapters of soul's experience living human life through the lens of your personality and conditioning, then you put yourself in a position to view both the process of life and the inevitability of death in new light. I invite you to live your life to the fullest in all that this means to you as a preparation for your eventual death. *You are headed for death, but I want you to live into a sense of being alive, factoring in that all of your time during this life can be used in intentional ways.* Your life is a chapter in the multilife journey of your soul and your death is, frankly, merely a punctuation point. It is in fact one of many punctuation points along the way and it need not be the awful, frightening, and traumatic experience that it seems to promise to be for those who are not ever really accepting that it is inevitable and will at some point come to them.

What does it mean to live life to the fullest? I have two answers for you. The first is to allow the process of creating meaning as described in a section above to unfold. This is to say to allow yourself to be yourself, express what is in you to express, and uncover the gift that your existence is here to give. There is no punishment for not doing this but it is in the heart of All That Is that you as a portion of it figure out how to become the source of love. Along the way this means feeding the loving part of yourself with experiences that you need to open up to love.

This means that you are challenged over time to honor who you are and bring out your unique self in order to give the gift of yourself in whatever form it naturally seeks to exist. When you honor who you are then you open to love – to being love. The gift you as a portion of divine consciousness came here to embody naturally finds its way to expression. So many of you live in fear of what might happen to you that you might not feel free to be open to what life has to offer you that is wonderful and what you have to offer life that is equally as wonderful. The first sections of this text are intended to give you some context about the life process and how all that you experience is in fact your creation and cocreation so that you can see more about how to work with the elements and dynamics of your life in an empowered way. If you do not see how to be empowered with what exists in your sphere, you will certainly not feel open to being empowered to do what you came here to do! It simply is not possible to live your soul's loving mission from a place of fear and with dread about what might happen to you next because of what has happened to you in the past.

The second answer is that you must go through a process to rewrite why the most important things that have occurred to and around you that have deeply affected you have happened. You must revise the history – the narrative you and your clever, protection-focused mind have attached to the facts of what has happened to create a sense of meaning about it and how you feel as a result of what happened – to reflect the logic of soul. Remember that this way of looking at your life centers on the fact that you have vibrated your life experiences into existence in order to show you more about who you are and where you are in the process of learning what love is, where it comes from, and who is responsible for giving it to whom. The logic of soul opens the door for you to own what you have experienced as useful for your divine journey to learn through human living what it means to become a being who chooses to generate love as a regular mode.

To die consciously you must own your life experiences as your creation. And this means *all* of your life experiences. You must revisit major junction points in your emotional history as the human you are and own what has happened. And you must do so not in terms of the judgment that is so easy for you to mete out upon yourself for having done something wrong if you or another has been injured through choices you made at that time. You must give yourself and all others involved in those narratives the benefit of the doubt that each of you is a long-term, multilife work in progress. I invite you to see all of this history as contributing to the evolution of consciousness as All That Is explores human living, and I invite you to do so without judgment of yourself and other. If you blame yourself for something in your past that has hurt you then you are not open to love. Similarly if you blame someone in your past for something that has hurt you, you cannot be open to love. Simple, straightforward forgiveness does do great things when applied well. But I want you not to merely let go of what has hurt you. I want you to understand it as your cocreation and to get to the point at which you can graciously accept that all that has hurt you in fact occurred for a reason and that the reason was not to punish or harm you. I want you to get to the point with this material I am sharing here that you are able to stand up in the middle of all the pain you have experienced at your own hand and the hands of others and own all of it. When you can do this you begin to step into a piece of your divine power that has been lacking in the lives of humans for as long as humans have existed. You have been trying to figure out why pain happens and hurt unfolds. Now I am coming through to share with you that all of it has been your cocreation and this, in fact, is something to celebrate. You-as-divine source are doing what you came here to do.

In one sense, dying is an opportunity to return to the place from which love comes. While embodied you are challenged over many lives to learn to be the source of love for yourself but your nature as All That Is is to *be* the source of love. In fact All That Is is commonly referred to as Source! When a human dies the context of normal human perception and the limits on the size and scope of consciousness is invited to give way to reconnect with love. This happens through the predeceased loved ones and guidance team who hold space for the newly-separated consciousness to adapt to being surrounded by loving support at all times. It is true that the task for the newly-departed consciousness is to open to love, and it certainly can be a difficult one as all manner of human perceptions, judgments, criticisms, and blame must be met and evaluated before being shed in favor of adapting to the logic of soul that is taught to the newly-departed during the orientation process.

Going through your history and rewriting the narrative of what has occurred will lead you to be able to fully occupy the present moment. It will set up your view on what is happening now as an extension of all those things that have been happening your entire life to teach you about how to become a loving being – how to become the source of love. If after working to rewrite your existing narratives about the past and what all of it meant you are still unclear about why your life is the way it is now, then you will need to apply the same process to what exists in your sphere now. Ultimately I am suggesting that living consciously in a way that prepares you consciously for death means to live in the present moment and engage with all that exists in your life in a meaningful way. But it took this entire book to get here because I had to show you a number of important things about how your consciousness, ideas, and beliefs about life become shaped through experience. I had to take you on a tour of how All That Is sets human existence into motion and then steps into it with the intention of forgetting its true nature as the source of love in order to attempt to remember it while in human form and come to embody its power as the source of love. You had to see what gets in the way of living a meaningful life and receive numerous invitations to let go of the need or habit to judge yourself for your choices and for what you have experienced over your years lived on Earth. But if you live in the present moment and appreciate all that comes to you as reflecting your multilife empowerment journey as All That Is playing at being human in order that you learn how to become the source of love while in human form, then you're getting it. In this case you would be living consciously in a way that paves the way for dying consciously and returning to the source of love as it is held and nurtured by All That Is when you are between lives.

I invite you to understand that as you are a complex and multilayered energetic being experiencing life emotionally, I want you to be easy on yourself when you think you have rewritten your history and then something later comes up with a tinge of bitterness, pain, guilt, shame, or regret. I want to be clear that energy moves through your consciousness and therefore your body in waves and that these waves ebb and flow. Energies in the form of emotions come to the surface when something in your thoughts, feelings, or environment echo something from the past that imprinted you negatively and inspired part of you to create a narrative in order to ensure that you can avoid recreating pain in the future. Something in your environment at some point might trigger you, in other words, and you may feel you have done wonderful work going through this text and altering your perspective in the ways that I have described. When this happens it is not that you have not done wonderful work to evolve and grow. It is because energies and emotions move through all different layers of your consciousness – and therefore body – and it is normal and natural to be triggered by something even after effective healing work has been done. The effect will be less than it was in the past before you put conscious awareness on something to transform your relationship with it. Once you own your experiences when an emotion is triggered you will find that the impact is more like an echo than opening an old wound. You will be able to stay grounded and in your body – intentional and clear in the moment – and more quickly and effectively move through it to come back to centered and present. And you will be ready to view this echoing resonance through the lens of love, which is to say compassion and self-acceptance. You will be more understanding of yourself as a divine work in progress. You will love having the opportunity to withhold self-judgment and shrug off guilt, shame, and regret.

Below are some questions to work with as you go through the process of becoming present, of becoming aware of being the source of love in your world, with some guidelines and tips to navigating what can come up for many humans when working with the information contained in this volume. Approached intentionally, they can serve as exercises to work through some issues that arise for humans when considering all that has been written in this book thus far.

What will you let pain mean to you? How will you conceive of what life is supposed to be like? Emotional and other kinds of pain are available in spades to people who are in a process of learning to deal with it. All humans experience such difficulty at times. It is up to you how you view the situations in your life that bring pain as they unfold. You will be put in difficult situations and, sometimes, feel firmly lodged between rocks and hard places. Dilemmas will come to you and impossible choices will, too. It is in your power to choose how you will conceive of why these things happen and your decision will in large part determine your experience of such situations when they come to and rise up within you. You are not a sheep who has incarnated to live a life on Earth being lead around with an ideal experience of idyllic placidness, being told what to do and doing it and having everything unfold peacefully, surrounded by gleefully chirping birds and sunbeams and rainbows. You are a portion of the creator consciousness, All That Is, the being that makes things happen! Your life is a reflection of what your soul needs to create, watch, feel, resist, and roll with in order to learn about what it takes to live human life and navigate the world of emotions and everything else. You are not here to seek a peaceful path upon which you need learn nothing. Far from it! You are here to sample all the possible drama and intensity available to humans along a multilife journey so they can learn to become the source of love. You are here to feel all manner of joy and pain and walk through it with conscious awareness and, in time, own all of it as your creation. As I mentioned above, this includes learning that others will not and cannot love you in the ways that you need to be loved. You in fact draw others to you who cannot meet your needs for feeling loved, supported, and safe because you as a piece of Goddess and God are here to learn to do those things for yourself as you learn to remember how to become the source of love while in human form.

Will you open to see multiple perspectives as to why things happen to and within you? You are in complete control as to how you view and interpret what happens around and within you. Many of you are not sure you have any bit of control over your lives but I wish for you to see that you become empowered as All That Is living human lives when you open to see the lens through which you view the world as a creative product of you-as-All That Is. What comes to you will reflect the logic of soul – what kinds of experiences you have as a person – and your response to them determines your experience. When something difficult comes to or rises up within you, are you willing to learn to see the value in it? Are you willing to breathe intentionally into that pain or tension and know that you are safe and that this is coming to or up within you for a good reason? Dying consciously is an outgrowth of living consciously. And that takes seeing all that comes to you as reflective of what you-as-soul, you-as-All That Is, have incarnated as you to learn. Living consciously takes recognizing your divine power as a creative being making all things that come to you happen.

Are you willing to grow older consciously? Are you willing to age with conscious intent? You are aging and, until you die, you will continue to age. Yet you have the choice in how you approach these facts. Your human culture has certain opinions about age and those who are aging that are in fact reflective of your collective conceptions of and experiences with death and dying. You value youth because you are afraid of dying, of stepping into the great unknown with the main variable being that you are not sure you will be welcomed with loving, open arms by anyone when and after you die. You are afraid that you have not lived well or been a good enough person and that someone is waiting to punish you after death. This is where the emphasis on youth and beauty and looking and seeming young comes from! Sometimes an older person in full acceptance of many truths described in this book will come along and have a calm, grounded statement to make about life and death. You allow yourselves to be temporarily inspired and then go back to dreading the thought of aging and eventually dying because you have not yet learned or, perhaps, accepted that each individual can make of life what he or she will. You are not in control of all of the details of your life and you cannot avoid the death of your body, but you are in complete control as to how you approach and work with the circumstances of your life including the aging process. To go with the above questions: *Are you willing to define who you are and shed the power of the collective fear about aging and what it means? Are you willing to be present with your experience of aging and own it?* It is up to you to shed the stranglehold cultural ideals about aging and dying may have on you.

Are you willing to learn to forgive yourself for all that has seemed a mistake or failure? How you choose to view why and how events have occurred are, as mentioned above, keys to your creative power as a portion of All That Is living a human life. Do what you can to accept that all humans experience what amounts to not measuring up to an external standard at least sometimes in their lives. If you put all of your ability to accept and feel good about yourself in the direction of measuring up to external standards, you will not see that you are in fact powerful as a loving being. You may not feel clear to get to your heart to begin simply accepting who you are and enjoying this moment of your life. You will not be able to forgive others for anything if you cannot forgive yourself. And if you cannot forgive others, you cannot effectively own your history and step into your power as a divine being playing at being human. It all begins with giving yourself the benefit of the doubt that you are a divine work in progress doing all you can to learn to become the source of love. If you are not being so for yourself, how could you possibly expect to be such a source for anyone else? I mean to say that if you cannot treat yourself with kindness, what do you think you are in fact vibrating toward and with others when you are trying to be loving? I encourage you in the strongest possible terms to choose to become the source of love for yourself so that you can give the gift of you to the world around you. It all begins with how you choose to view yourself, your choices, and your worth.

Are you willing to make peace with the present and accept what is? Are you willing to make peace with the past and accept what has been? To own what All That Is has created through you, a portion of it having forgotten the big picture and your power, is to move toward owning your power. You have been creating all along. You have always been powerful.

You have been making all of this happen and there is a wonderful reason for it! You are, after all, learning with the help of many other portions of All That Is to become loving.

Finally, are you willing to adapt to the presence of the logic of soul in your human life? This is to ask if you are prepared to gracefully accept what comes to you and, from a grounded place, work consciously with all the variables at play in your heart, mind, and life to find a solution. Here's a little hint: All problems that come to you point at the need for you to become the source of love. Along the way you go through much that is to be filed under "what love is, where it comes from, and who's responsible for giving it to whom." In one way or another, all of it reveals that others cannot love you in the ways that you need.

Thus far you have not seen that the solution to working through the manifestations of the logic of soul in your life – what comes to and up within you that's difficult and/or painful – can be brought to resolution if you step more in the direction of becoming the source of love. Up to this point you have perhaps not realized that you are a portion of the divine creative intelligence that has brought all things into existence and is making all of this happen. Well, now you know. Now you have the whole story about why the world around you unfolds as it does. I leave it to you to explore accepting your divine role in all that has happened and is happening to you now and step into your power as the source of love.

Thank you for your time, attention, and energy. It has been a pleasure sharing this information with you.

About Djehuty

Djehuty (a.k.a. Thoth, St. Germain, and Merlin) is an ascended master. He has been made a mythological and/or deified figure in all Earth cultures. He represents the Hermes archetype – translator, teacher, scribe, and mediator. His commitment is to serve humanity by teaching humans how to evolve and move toward the evolutionary goal of the manifestation experiment: Learning in human form to remember their divine nature as the source of love.

About the Channel

Tom Jacobs is an Evolutionary Astrologer and Channel. A graduate of Evolutionary Astrologer Steven Forrest's Apprenticeship Program, Tom has a global practice of readings, coaching, and tutoring to help people understand what they came to Earth to do and supporting them in making it happen. He is the author and channel of books on astrology, mythology, and spirituality and original astrological natal reports on Lilith and 2012 & emotional healing. Tom also hosts the popular weekly radio show The Soul's Journey on Contact Talk Radio.

Contact Tom Jacobs via http://tdjacobs.com.

Made in the USA
San Bernardino, CA
24 February 2016